FINDING SEEKERS

How to Develop
a Spiritual Direction Practice
from Beginning to Full-Time Employment

BRUCE TALLMAN

the apocryphile press
BERKELEY, CA
www.apocryphile.org

apocryphile press | www.apocryphile.org
BERKELEY, CA | VANCOUVER, BC

APOCRYPHILE PRESS
In the US: 1700 Shattuck Ave #81
Berkeley, CA 94709

In Canada: #359-1917 West 4th Avenue
Vancouver, B.C. Canada V6J-1M7

To my mother
Alice Tallman
who taught me the meaning
of unconditional love

OTHER BOOKS BY BRUCE TALLMAN

Archetypes for Spiritual Direction:
Discovering the Heroes Within
(2005, Paulist Press | ISBN: 0-8091-4358-5)

Table of Contents

Acknowledgements

I would first of all like to acknowledge my mother, Alice Tallman, a most sweet and kind lady who always created harmony in our family when I was growing up. Besides teaching me the meaning of unconditional love, she taught me that we are free to go our own way and do what we believe is right for us. By marrying my father, Fred Tallman, who was paraplegic, she even had to go against the wishes of her parents. Her decision to follow her own lights was justified when Dad proved her right by becoming an extremely successful businessman. Perhaps I have been fortunate enough to inherit a small part of his wisdom, which has come in very handy in my present work.

I think most people who knew me thought I had taken leave of my senses in 2002 when I said I wanted to be a full-time spiritual director, but I had to go my own way and do what I felt was right for me. In fact, I feel like I had no choice, since this was clearly the direction my Higher Power was calling me to. So far it has been a pretty wild ride, with my faith being tested every step of the way, but my Higher Power has not let me down yet.

Besides my parents, I want to thank my wife Grace for her constant love, support, and encouragement. "We're in this together, *n'est ce pas?*"

I would also like to thank the following people for their invaluable editorial work on this book:

Sabrina Caldwell, former Board Member of the Pacific Jubilee Program in Spiritual Directors Training and presently Lead Minister of a Presbyterian Church in Peterborough, Ontario, and Miriam Frey, Chairperson of the Steering Committee of Spiritual Directors of Ontario and Executive Committee Member of Spiritual Directors International. Miriam's tough editing and Sabrina's astute observations played a large role in my rewriting of this book.

As well, I am grateful to John Mabry, publisher of Apocryphile Press and Editor of *Presence*, the primary journal of Spiritual Directors International, for five years of its existence. *Finding Seekers* had been selling well as an ebook since 2007, but John thought it should be made available in paperback form as well. I appreciate very much his prompting on this.

The explosion of social media since 2007 has also necessitated the revising and updating of the book. When I first made *Finding Seekers* available as an ebook, Facebook and YouTube were just starting, and Twitter was unknown. The basic principle of *Finding Seekers* still holds true—that is, who knows you hires you—but now there are so many ways to become known beyond putting together snappy brochures, doing workshops, and face-to-face networking. With the advent of Skype, it is now possible to do spiritual direction with people thousands of miles away, while sitting in the comfort of your home office. I now have directees in California, Cape Cod, Philadelphia, New York, and Quebec, and my own spiritual director lives in Denver, Colorado.

We are entering into a whole new era of possibilities for spiritual direction. My belief is that, as spiritual directors discover with the help of *Finding Seekers* that they can make spiritual direction their primary employment, the field of spiritual direction will explode just as the social media have, and usher in a new and much needed spiritual era for our whole planet. Right from the start that has been my hope and vision for this book.

SECTION A

For Beginners and Part-Time Spiritual Directors and Counselors

CHAPTER ONE

The Spirituality of Developing a Spiritual Direction Practice

What everyone wants, including the seventy or eighty percent of the population that no longer attends church regularly, is absolute love, peace, and joy. Nothing less will totally satisfy them. In other words, what everyone really wants, whether they know it or not, is God, Absolute Bliss-Consciousness, the Great Spirit, or however you conceive the Higher Power to be. (Since "God" is a loaded word for some people, I will just use "Higher Power" throughout the book.)

Basically, everyone is called to be a lover of their Higher Power. As spiritual "directors," "guides," or "counselors" (I will be using these terms interchangeably) we are called to help people satisfy this deepest want, need, longing, and desire. What a glorious calling! To sustain this calling and develop a spiritual direction practice, you need a solid spiritual basis.

First of all, it is your Higher Power who builds your spiritual direction practice. Without your Higher Power you are building in vain. A spiritual direction practice obviously must be Spirit-based. Without the action of the Higher Power within you, your practice will go nowhere. It all comes from, and goes to, the Higher Power.

Secondly, your practice must be built upon prayer. Your primary activity must be prayer, contemplation, and meditation. You can ask your Higher Power to lead people to you, and ask others to pray for you. At the end of each spiritual direction session, if appropriate, I tell my seekers that I will keep them in my prayers, and I ask them to pray for me. I pray for them individually Monday to Friday, and I pray for them as a group on the weekend. This way I am always praying for them, and I always have thirty to forty people praying for me. I don't specifically ask them to pray that my practice goes well, but I believe that it is their prayers, more than anything else, that is the secret of my practice staying alive.

Your Higher Power and prayer build your practice, and you build it. There is a universal spiritual law found in every major religion, the law of giving and receiving. In eastern religions it is called "karma." Jesus taught that as you sow you reap. Basically, it means that what you give you get back, sooner or later. In fact, you usually get back more than you give because the Higher Power multiplies your efforts.

There are two basic mistakes in building a spiritual direction practice: to do everything and expect your Higher Power to do nothing, and to do nothing and expect your Higher Power to do everything. Your practice is a genuine partnership between you and your Higher Power, a genuine co-creation.

Also, spiritual values build your practice. To paraphrase Jesus again: "Put your Higher Power first in your life, and your Higher Power, who knows everything you need, will take care of all your needs."

As a spiritual counselor, you may believe, as I did, that money is a vile thing, and something you can ignore. However money, in and of itself, is morally neutral, neither good nor bad. The way money works and the way good business works is according to this formula: "money follows trust, relationships, love, service, and putting people first."

In other words, money and good business follow spiritual values. Let me explain.

We tend to give our money to those we trust. If your car breaks down, do you take it to the garage where they overcharge you, do unnecessary repairs, and get you to spend as much as possible, or do you take it to the garage where you trust the staff because they treat their customers in a friendly and fair way, and seem to have your best interests at heart? A spiritual counseling practice is all about loving people and building relationships with them. People tend to go where they feel loved. In fact, they will drive long distances to experience their spiritual counselor's love.

People also tend to go where they get the best service for their dollar. If you consistently go the extra mile with your clients and give them above average service, they will consistently come to you.

If you genuinely put people first, before money, people will sense this, trust you, and gladly pay for your services. However, if you put money before people, they will see through your attempts to manipulate them, and will not return.

It is doing things according to spiritual values of love, trust, service, and putting people first that makes for a sustainable, ongoing practice.

In summary, it is your Higher Power, prayer, your efforts, and doing things according to spiritual values that builds a thriving spiritual direction or counseling practice.

CHAPTER TWO

The Ethics of Developing
a Spiritual Direction Practice

Quite simply, if you put ethics first in your spiritual guidance practice, everything else will be taken care of. If you put ethics first, you will build a good reputation, people will trust you, and referrals and money will follow. However, there are many subtle ways you can violate ethical principles.

It is tempting to make extravagant claims about your services: "Spiritual guidance will transform your entire life." This may happen, but the potential client should be informed that it may take years and years.

Another common temptation is to misrepresent your qualifications. Misrepresentation can easily happen with certificates, since you can be given a certificate for participating in a one day, weekend, month long, or two year program. There are people out there claiming to be "certified spiritual counselors" who only took a week long workshop. The wife of one of my friends recently hung out her shingle saying "Intuitive Direction" even though she has absolutely no training in spiritual direction. Another acquaintance, who was running a small consulting business for churches, put "Ed.D., D. Min." after his name, giving the impression that his diplomas in education and ministry were really doctorates.

It can also be tempting to manipulate clients. There are a thousand subtle ways to do this: withholding information, scheduling unnecessary sessions, not referring them to other counselors when those other counselors could help your client more than you could in a particular area, having your clients do personality typologies when they came to you struggling with their image of God or the sudden death of their child. You constantly have to ask yourself as a spiritual guide: "Am I giving this person what *they need* or what *I want* them to work on?" Every spiritual counselor will benefit from having a supervisor who helps them be aware of temptations and clarify what their hidden motivations are. Misrepresenting your qualifications or manipulating clients is always based on the fear that "I am not good enough" or "I will not have enough."

The solution to all these ethical temptations is to trust your Higher Power, to remind yourself that if your Higher Power genuinely called you to this, then your Higher Power will give you the means to make it happen, so be at peace. "Where the Higher Power guides, the Higher Power provides" is a good slogan for the fledgling spiritual director, guide, or counselor.

A lot can also be learned by studying the ethical guidelines given to psychologists and social workers by their regulating bodies, that is, their professional associations. To be a registered psychologist for example, you have to agree that the marketing of your services will be done according to *professional*, not *commercial* standards.

Professional standards mean that your brochures just *describe* your services, they don't *evaluate* them. A professional psychologist is not allowed to say, for example, that "We guarantee your depression will be cured."

Psychologists are also not allowed to use testimonials from their clients in their brochures. For example, "Our sex life is the best it's ever been since we went to see Dr. Davidoff." Testimonials are usually a problem anyway, because if you include the full name of the person giving the testimonial, it will appear as a breach of confidentiality, even if you asked the testifier for permission to use their name. And if you don't include the name of the testifier, people who read the brochure may think you just made the testimonials up.

Perhaps a half way measure, if you want to use testimonials, would be to just use people's initials.

You also violate professional standards if you pay people in any way for referring people to you. You, as a spiritual counselor, cannot work out private "deals." These kind of deals are not uncommon in the business world. For example, someone who installs prefab kitchens might pay people who sell these kitchens ten percent of his salary if they refer their customers to him. Obviously this would not be acceptable in spiritual counseling.

By far the best ethical guidelines for spiritual directors and counselors have been developed by Spiritual Directors International in their booklet "Guidelines for Ethical Conduct." The following is a summary of key parts of these guidelines and my reflections on them.

First of all, your primary ethical responsibility in running a spiritual direction practice is, as I wrote earlier, to sincerely love your clients. If your clients feel loved by you, they will keep coming back, and they will spread the word about you to others. Not all clients will stay, but if you show them that you sincerely love them, you will eventually have a solid base of ongoing clients.

Secondly, you must respect all persons regardless of race, color, sex, sexual orientation, age, ethnic background, social status, religion, and so on. Spiritual directors must show God's grace and mercy to all.

Third, treat your clients justly at all times. Any kind of manipulation of clients will eventually be detected by them, causing them to quit. So, do not abuse your clients in any way. This can include:

- spiritual abuse, by not respecting their spirituality, theology, conscience, religious experiences, religious tradition, confidentiality, etc.

- emotional abuse, by trying to belittle them, or by coercing people to come to you, to stay with you, or to do what you want

- financial abuse, by over-charging or over-scheduling appointments

- physical abuse, by not respecting boundaries.

You have to give people the freedom to be in charge of their own process, including the decision to come and go as they please. Spirit works by way of freedom. The Higher Power must be the center and director of the sessions. Otherwise you are usurping the place of God, a sure recipe for disaster. My worst sessions are always the ones where I think I am the spiritual director, not God.

Fourth, be competent. Get as much training in spiritual counseling as possible, and keep learning.

Fifth, take care of your own needs outside of the spiritual counseling relationship. Constantly work on your own spiritual development, get any therapy you need, have your own spiritual director to guide you, and partake of either individual or peer group supervision.

Sixth, maintain a good relationship with the leaders of your own spiritual tradition and respect those in other traditions. Be genuinely ecumenical.

For more depth and details about the "Guidelines For Ethical Conduct," contact Spiritual Directors International at office@ sdiworld.org. Every spiritual director and counselor should be familiar with this booklet.

If you are an ethical, caring, just, and competent spiritual director, word-of-mouth—the best advertising there is—will spread quickly and build your practice for you. People tend to believe what *others* say about you more than they believe what *you* say about you. If someone who has no vested interest says you are a good spiritual counselor, that means infinitely more than anything you could say about yourself.

CHAPTER THREE

Finding Seekers: General Principles

Prayer, Meditation, And Affirmations

I believe that the key thing in finding clients is prayer. When I pray about my practice I usually start with a prayer of gratitude for any blessings in the past week. An attitude of gratitude creates a mind-set of abundance, and an abundance mentality combined with gratitude seems to open us up to even more of our Higher Power's blessings in a "blessing circle" that never ends. This is the polar opposite to a vicious circle.

I then admit to my Higher Power and myself that I cannot build my practice without my Higher Power's help, and then ask my Higher Power to send me new clients so that they may grow spiritually. Next, I pray that all my past and present clients will spiritually grow. Finally, I pray for each of my present clients individually, and for their specific spiritual needs. Usually I have about forty clients, so this can take a bit of time.

You could also use imaginative meditation and affirmations. You could imagine how you would feel if you had a waiting list of clients, or imagine the phone constantly ringing with people wanting to take spiritual direction. You could also say your spiritual mission out loud and with feeling as an affirmation: "By the grace of my Higher Power, I help many people grow spiritually."

Building A Wide Referral Base

Besides trusting my Higher Power, the only other source of any feeling of security I find in this work is to have a wide referral base. If you have many different people who refer clients to you, it can be the source of stability and longevity in your practice. Having a steady flow of clients will help you avoid ebbs and flows in your practice. It is the ebbs, the times when you are losing clients and not gaining new ones, that cause spiritual counselors self-doubt. When you start to wonder if things will ever flow again, it is easy to get discouraged and think about quitting.

There are people out there who interact with lots of other people. They may spend a significant amount of time listening to people express their wants, needs, and problems, and could refer these people to you. Besides church staff, other people who could be key referral sources are doctors, lawyers, human resource managers, hair dressers, massage therapists, teachers, psychologists, social workers, financial planners, and even bartenders. If you keep track of where your referrals come from you can focus on developing those sources even more.

If you develop your practice properly and nourish your referral sources, you will find that clients will eventually come to you without a lot of stress and strain on your part. The key to building a practice is building relationships, not beating the bushes looking for clients.

In fact, high pressure selling and self-promotion usually don't work in the long run because these things make you look desperate and send a message that your services are inadequate on their own merits in attracting clients. It also gives the impression that you are willing to compromise your integrity by exaggerating the efficacy of your services.

Once a referral source is in place, you just need to tend it now and then to keep the referrals coming. It is important to build and maintain good relationships with everyone: besides the people mentioned above, there are agency directors, agency or church secretaries, participants in your talks or workshops, and so on. In general, "referrals follow relationships."

If you get to know who are the local experts in a wide variety of fields you could refer clients to them if the client has a need or problem in a particular area. This is an extra service you can provide for clients, and these experts may start to refer people to you. I have had several clients whose doctors said to them that nothing more could be done medically and encouraged their patient to find a good spiritual director.

The wise spiritual director or counselor will stay connected to the leaders in their own religious or spiritual tradition as a likely source of clients. They will also reach out to others in other religious or spiritual traditions; that is, the wise spiritual director will work ecumenically. Back in the day, spiritual direction used to be mainly a Catholic practice, but now people in many other Christian denominations are becoming familiar with it, as are people from other major religious traditions such as Buddhism and Judaism. In fact, people often like to see a spiritual director or counselor from outside their own denomination or tradition for reasons of confidentiality or to learn new spiritual methods and ideas.

Word-Of-Mouth

Most therapists, doctors, and lawyers agree that word-of-mouth was the key to the success of their practice. It all begins with words: the words that come out of your mouth: in your sessions with clients, and in talks and workshops you give. Based on your competence and caring, clients and participants will talk to others, and those people will talk to people they know, who will talk to others who have no direct connection to you at all.

I caught myself telling someone once that I heard Murray Watson was a very good professor. I then realized that I had never had any direct contact with Watson, but I had heard about his abilities through someone else. When I asked that "someone else" how they knew Watson was so good, they said they had heard it from someone else!

If five clients each tell five other people you are a good spiritual director, and those twenty-five people each tell five other people, and those one hundred and twenty-five people each tell five other people, you will soon have six hundred and twenty-five people singing your praises! Word-of-mouth is what I call "the wildfire effect."

The biggest benefit to you is that, as I wrote earlier, people tend to trust what *others* say about you more than what *you* say about you for the simple reason that you have an obvious vested interest in saying good things about you. Word-of-mouth is so powerful because it spreads so fast and because people trust it. This is why, in an era of no phones, text messages, or email, Jesus and the Buddha had thousands of people following them around. Now that we have these things, plus Twitter and Facebook, things can go viral even more quickly. In fact, word-of-text may be even more powerful than word-of-mouth.

Constant Recruitment, Repetition, And Reaching Out

Constant recruiting is the name of the game. I am not advocating aggressive marketing here, but simply the never-ending process of following new leads, trying new things, and developing new referral sources.

Unfortunately (or fortunately depending on how you look at it), you never totally "arrive" when developing a spiritual direction or counseling practice. Even psychologists and social workers who have a wide referral base and have been running their own practice for twenty years have told me the cliche that "you are only as good as your last session." You never get to just rest and relax and feel like your practice is forever secure. Our only real security lies in our Higher Power.

To use one more cliche, "if you are not going forward you are going backward." This is because your clients will all, at some point, drop out. Even the ones you consider to be your most faithful clients, and who have been with you for years, will one day decide to move on. Often, it is when you finally make progress with someone, and they finally get what they came for, that they will then decide to quit or move on.

Once a person decides they want to go, you cannot hold them, and if you try to, it will mean you will eventually part anyway, and not on the best terms. So try to say goodbye on positive terms, since last impressions are lasting. If you review the person's progress with them, and let them go gracefully, they will be one of your strongest advocates. And remember the wildfire effect.

Sometimes a potential referral source will need several exposures to you and your basic message before they will respond. At first, you might need to connect with them in some way once a month for six months in order to remind them you are out there and available. Peoples' memories need to be periodically refreshed about your vision, your services, and your openings.

Timing has a great deal to do with finding seekers. You may not be the very best spiritual director or counselor in a city, but if you have recently contacted an agency director, priest, minister, or secretary, you will be fresh on their mind and they will be more likely to refer people to you since you have recently contacted them. They will more likely refer a person to you rather than to the very best spiritual director whom they have not heard from or thought of in months.

Once your referral source responds and sends you someone, thank them graciously and profusely. You also need to thank and cultivate your established referral sources. As with your most faithful clients, your most faithful referral sources will at some point move on. They may move to a different city, retire, become ill, or reorganize their services, and you may never hear from them again. So it is important to not only nurture your present referral sources, but also to constantly search for new ones.

Remember that God wants us to show love to others, and you may be God's providence to someone. People often say to me "It was so providential that you called" or "That workshop you did was just what I needed to hear, at just the right time." The key thing is to reach out in love. There are so many people out there who could be helped immensely by a good spiritual director.

The great Protestant clergyman, Robert Schuller, started his vast ministry by simply going door-to-door in his neighborhood and asking people how the church could help them. In my diocese, the Catholic Diocese of London, Ontario, there is a similar story. Wherever Father Jim Williams went, the parish would thrive. His secret? When he was in active ministry, he would spend at least an hour every day visiting every household within his parish boundaries, whether Catholic or not.

Now, I am not advocating going door-to-door, but research on church growth shows that it is a very interpersonal process. Most people come to know their Higher Power through another human being, usually a family member (most often their mother or father) or a close friend. The church mainly grows by word-of-mouth, by one person talking to another. That's how the early church grew, and the same principle applies to building a spiritual direction or counseling practice today. Finding seekers is a very interpersonal process.

Clearly Communicating Your Message

When you are trying to attract people you need to convey your deep conviction about the value of spiritual direction. You must be able to clearly and concisely state what you do. The more complicated or technical you are in your explanation of your work, the more you will turn people off. For example, if someone asks you what you do in spiritual direction, and you say something like "I do the Nineteenth Annotation from a Jungian perspective," you will draw a puzzled look from most people. The vast majority of listeners would think "What on earth is she talking about?"

If you seem uncomfortable in explaining what you do, it will be a warning flag for most people, and they will probably not make further inquiries. However, if someone asks what you do and you smile, make eye contact with them, and say "I'm a spiritual counselor. I help people grow spiritually," there is so much interest in spirituality out there, people will probably ask "How do you do that?" or "Is that hard to do?" or "Is this just for church-goers?" or "What's that all about?" or "How did you get trained in that?" and so on. If you speak with enthusiasm about your work and say that you love it because it helps a lot of people, you will probably get more questions. You know you are speaking to a potential new client when they ask a lot of questions. Questions are a sign of genuine interest.

Some other tips about clear communication:

- tell them your full name if they don't already know it.

- don't mention "God" unless you sense your listener will feel comfortable with this. "God" and "church" and "Christ" and "religion" are loaded words for a lot of people.

- if you call yourself a "spiritual counselor," people are more likely to understand what you do.

People understand what counseling is, but they don't understand what "direction" is.

I don't call myself a "spiritual friend" or "spiritual companion" as some spiritual directors do, because it doesn't convey the professionalism of what I do, it sounds *too* intimate for someone who barely knows me, and the person is likely to think "Well, I have lots of spiritual friends and companions, I don't need another one who charges me money!"

- with some people, if you are Christian and call yourself a "Christian counselor," they are likely to run away because they know of "Christian counselors" who manipulate people with their fundamentalist knowledge of the Bible.

- keep your message short and to the point: two sentences you can say in fifteen seconds or less.

- write your message out, memorize it, practice it until you feel confident and professional, and then begin to say it at every opportunity, with individuals or groups.

- remember to pause after you explain what you do. This allows people to make comments or ask questions like "Do people find this therapeutic?" This keeps them engaged so you can tell them more and continue to build the relationship. Again, if they keep asking questions you know you are talking to a potential client.

- do not, I repeat, *do not* interject what you do or what spiritual direction is all about into one-to-one conversations or at parties unless someone first asks you. There is nothing worse than listening to someone at a party go on and on about the benefits they have experienced from some new herbal cure or some new therapeutic technique only to realize that this person is selling this product, and introduced it into the conversation merely as a sales pitch. On the other hand, I have recruited quite a few new clients without even trying just by responding clearly and concisely to their queries about what I do. I wasn't intending to sell them on spiritual direction, I was just having a conversation with them and was surprised when they suggested coming to see me.

Normal conversations when riding in the car with a group of people, when on an airplane, or at a party, workshop, or meeting can be a fruitful source of recruitment as long as you are clear about what you do. It is also a good idea to carry business cards you can hand out if someone asks for your contact information, but again, don't start off the conversation by handing out your card and telling them what you do. Wait for their questions. Otherwise it will sound like an artificial sales pitch instead of a natural conversation.

Another potential source of clients, besides people you meet in your daily life, is the significant others of your clients. Every client has a whole web of people they are in contact with on a regular basis: spouses, friends, relatives, co-workers, fellow church-goers or spiritual seekers or service club members, and so on. You might make a computer-generated certificate that entitles the holder to a free hour of spiritual direction or spiritual counseling, and then give five of these to each of your clients to pass on to others as gifts for birthdays, weddings or other occasions. You could also donate these to churches or other organizations holding silent auctions or fund-raisers. You would not receive any monetary reward, but gift certificates like this can be a good way to have people sample and learn about your services, and some may want to continue on a paying basis. If they don't, consider the free session to be a gift or a tithe of your services to a fellow seeker.

Reaching Out By Phone

Back in 1985, I was selected by my church to be the leader of "Renew," a church spiritual renewal process. It was necessary to find people to serve on the ten committees of Renew.

When I began phoning people in the church to ask them if they were interested in being on a committee, I found there were three basic responses people gave:

- I could serve, but am not interested
- I want to serve, but I can't due to other commitments
- I can serve and I want to.

So, I was able to recruit about every third person I phoned.

When I was a spiritual direction intern, we had to do ninety hours of free spiritual direction as part of our practicum. I thought "How am I going to find enough directees to complete this requirement?" Then I remembered my experience with Renew. So, I made a list of thirty people I knew, called them and told them what I was doing. I received a similar response:

- I can, but I don't want to
- I want to, but I can't
- I can and I want to.

Consequently, I recruited ten people and easily completed the practicum requirement.

You have to make an internal judgement, of course, as to who you feel comfortable calling and when you might be stepping over the line and getting into a "dual" relationship, that is, you are mixing spiritual direction with friendship. An interesting point, however, is that the people I felt closest to were most often not interested anyway, whereas the people I knew the least were often the ones who said "yes, I'm interested." So don't be shy about calling people who you barely know.

I once visited a man who had been running his own grief counseling practice for about three years. He was doing quite well at it, and I wanted to know how he marketed his services. He said that "building a practice is a very interpersonal process. Interacting with people beats paperwork every time. You can have the snappiest brochures and the best advertising in newspapers that money can buy, but it won't do you much good in getting clients."

In my own experience, asking people if they are interested in doing spiritual direction with me beats paperwork every time. I could mail them my brochures and they could read them and file them away with the intention of pondering at some point whether they would like to do spiritual direction or not. But when I phone them a week after I send the brochure, and ask them if they would be interested in giving spiritual direction a try, *they have to make a choice.* Paper does not require a response whereas directly asking does. Yes or no, I want to do spiritual direction or I don't.

So, try this. Make a list of all the people you know who you could phone to let them know that you are available for spiritual direction. First just ask if you can send them your brochure. Be sure to stress the benefits of spiritual direction in both the phone call and the brochure.

Here is how I have done this:

"Hi (say their first name: this tells them you are not a telemarketer). This is Bruce Tallman." (If they don't immediately know who you are, let them know how you know them. For example, "We were on the ecumenism committee together. Do you remember me now?")

"I am just calling because I have been working as a spiritual director for the past while, and although the people I work with say spiritual direction is very helpful in deepening their faith (stress the benefits up front), not many people know I am doing this, so I am just phoning to let people know I am out there.

"Do you know what spiritual direction is (their first name)?" If 'yes' go on. If 'no' explain that "It is basically spiritual counseling, although we are not doing therapy, we are just exploring your spiritual journey together.

"I was wondering if I could send you my spiritual direction brochure?" Ninety-five percent of people will say 'yes'. If 'yes,' ask them if they have email and if you can send them your email brochure. Note: your email brochure can be just ten or so lines about the benefits of spiritual direction. If 'no' they don't have email, say "Sending brochures by regular mail is time-consuming, so I am wondering if you really want to receive my brochure, or would it just be a waste of your time and my time?" If 'yes' they want to receive it, then get their address and tell them you will get it in the mail to them today. If 'no' they don't want to receive it, say "No problem. Let me know if you ever change your mind."

If you did mail or email your brochure to them, phone them a week or so later and ask if they got your email or regular mail brochure, if they had time to read it, if they have any questions, and if they would be interested in giving spiritual direction a try. If 'yes,' set up an appointment.

It takes a certain amount of courage to phone and ask someone if they are interested in spiritual direction, but it is helpful to remember that their response is both providential and circumstantial. Many people have told me that it was providential that I called because they were feeling the need for some spiritual guidance, and were hoping that God would send someone to them. Calling is also circumstantial and a "numbers game." If you call enough people you will inevitably find someone who is in the right circumstances to participate in spiritual direction. People always thanked me for calling, whether they were interested or not.

To call people you have to prepare yourself mentally. A key part of mental preparation is the attitude that, if people say they are not interested, they are not rejecting *you* personally, it is because of where *they* are at. In other words, it is about them, not about you. Success in calling people is not about how slick, aggressive, or persuasive you are. In fact, it's not about being slick, aggressive, or persuasive at all. It depends upon the Higher Power and the mind set and circumstances of the person you are calling.

So, just be yourself when you are calling, and if they are not interested, don't take it personally or get upset or depressed. By all means treat the other person with great respect. They may remember how polite you were to them and call you back later when they *are* ready to do spiritual direction, thinking "I know this person will treat me with dignity and won't try to force me to do things I don't want to do."

Get Brochures Out There

You may have some success with placing flyers/brochures in Christian or other spiritually-oriented bookstores. You can arrange with the bookstore manager to put your flyers/brochures near the cash register, and to have the flyers say that the *bookstore* offers its clients a free hour of spiritual direction or counseling. The inside of the flyer/brochure describes what spiritual direction is all about, the benefits of doing it, who you are, and your contact information. You benefit three ways: by the publicity, by people being exposed to your practice when they come to you, and by the people who decide to keep coming on a paid basis. Here is an example of a cover letter to a bookstore manager and the front panel of a brochure for bookstores:

Bookstore Cover Letter

Dear Natalia:

Hope business is brisk for you and most importantly that you have time yourself to prepare for Easter.

My name is Dr. Bruce Tallman. I have been working for the Diocese of London for the past 14 years as director of diocesan adult religious education centers in London and Sarnia. I recently completed a Doctor of Ministry Degree in Spiritual Direction and am working at present as a full-time spiritual director in London.

I was wondering if, as a bonus for your customers, you would be interested in displaying my flyers for a free one hour spiritual direction session with me, compliments of your store. Please see the enclosed flyer that Mustard Seed Bookstore displays in its store. Obviously, if you are interested I would change "Mustard Seed Bookstore" to "Peaceful Dove Book Store" on the front page of the flyer.

This would be a win-win-win situation. It would give your customers a free spiritual direction session, be a bonus for shopping at your store and might draw new people in, and expose them to my private practice. So, you, your customers, and myself would all benefit. Also, I will encourage my clients to use your store and I will mention your store (whenever appropriate) in talks, days of prayer, workshops, and courses I give. If people who take the flyers don't use them, they might pass them on to family and friends and thus advertise your store.

I will cover the cost of producing the flyers and supply two plastic holders for them, so there will be no cost to you.

If you are interested in discussing this, please call or email me and I will come and see you.

Sincerely,

Bruce Tallman, Dr. Min.

519-433-0981

email: btallman@rogers.com

web: www.brucetallman.com

Bookstore Brochure Front Panel

TAKE ONE

*THE
MUSTARD SEED
BOOK
STORE*

*offers you, your family, or friends
one FREE hour of*

SPIRITUAL DIRECTION

with this flyer

Another important place for your brochures is the brochure rack in most churches or other helping agencies. Ask the agency director or secretary, or the priest, pastor, or minister if it is okay for you to put your brochures out on a regular basis. Most churches and agencies have someone who removes unauthorized advertising from their bulletin boards and brochure racks, so if you put your brochures out without permission you may be wasting your time and money.

Most conferences on religious issues or spirituality have a table set aside that people can put their brochures and business cards on. This is a way for large crowds to freely swap information. Try to find out who is organizing the conference and ask if you can put your brochure out. In your brochure you can offer to do spiritual direction by phone or Skype with clients who live far away. There are phone plans that allow you to call anywhere in North America for free, so you don't have to charge long distance calls to your clients. Check these out with long distance providers in your area. Spiritual direction or counseling by phone has the disadvantage of lack of nonverbal clues given by the client but it has the advantage of pure listening, and can be almost as effective as being there in person.

You could also put brochures in grocery stores, convenience stores, laundromats, or any other place where people linger. Again, it should be authorized by someone that it is okay for you to leave brochures there, or they will probably be removed. You could also carry your business cards and a container of tacks with you wherever you go and post your cards on every bulletin board you pass in malls, bookstores, churches, etc. If your card has your website on it, people can go to it to find out lots more information about you. Or you could put a one page sheet explaining spiritual direction's benefits, with tear-off phone numbers, in the same locations.

It is important to respond to anyone who shows some interest with an email or snail mail cover letter and brochure stressing the benefits of spiritual direction. Here is a sample email cover letter and brochure:

Email Cover Letter

Dear (potential client's name),

Thank you for inquiring about spiritual direction. Most people I work with say that spiritual direction helps them to strengthen their faith, renew their prayer life, find greater direction in their life. It is particularly helpful for those experiencing a spiritual dry spell or struggling spiritually.

People often have specific issues or decisions they need to resolve and so just come for a few sessions. Or they may believe in the value of ongoing feedback throughout their spiritual life.

Some of my forty or so clients enjoy doing various popular spiritual growth programs with me such as *The Spiritual Exercises of St. Ignatius,* or *The Cup of Our Life* by Sr. Joyce Rupp or *Experiencing the Heart of Jesus* by Max Lucado. In our spiritual direction sessions we reflect on what they are experiencing with these workbooks, which they study on their own.

I maintain a resource library of DVDs and CDs that you can borrow at no cost to help you reflect on various spiritual topics at home. As well, every month I email to all my clients a new list of "Top Ten Ideas for Spiritual Growth."

All of the above is optional. We basically focus on whatever you want to work on for however long you want to come.

I try to accommodate people from different income levels, so fees

quency of sessions will be mutually determined at the first ses-
spiritual direction is very affordable, and we will be sure to
out a financial arrangement that you will feel comfortable with.

The attached brochure will familiarize you with spiritual direction. We will always proceed in a way and at a pace you feel comfortable with. Everyone is welcomed and accepted wherever they
are spiritually and with whatever they want to work on.

Peace and Blessings,

Dr. Bruce Tallman

Email Brochure

What Is Spiritual Direction All About?

Our Higher Power is the only real agent of growth in our lives.
The spiritual director is a trained listener, guide, and friend on your
spiritual journey and can be a layperson or ordained.

In the context of a safe, one-to-one, confidential relationship, you
meet with the spiritual director for one hour as often as you want,
and reflect on your spiritual journey.

You can attend as many or as few sessions as you like and share
as little or as much as you want. You are always in charge of your
own process of spiritual growth.

Benefits of Spiritual Direction

- gentle, non-judgemental guidance
- growth in faith, hope, love, and prayer in relation to feelings,
  family, work, choices, loss, forgiveness, illness and all life's
  spiritual struggles
- greater meaning and purpose in your life

The Spiritual Director

Bruce Tallman works as a full-time ecumenical spiritual director
in private practice. He is a member of Spiritual Directors
International and subscribes to their ethical standards and practices.

Bruce presents workshops and retreats across Canada and the
United States and has published numerous articles in both religious

and secular journals. His book *Archetypes for Spiritual Direction: Discovering the Heroes Within* was published by Paulist Press in September 2005.

Bruce holds a Doctor of Ministry Degree in Spiritual Direction from the Graduate Theological Foundation, affiliated with Oxford University. He is past director of adult religious education centers in London and Sarnia.

Bruce welcomes people of all beliefs and is committed to reverence for the dignity, equality, rights, and gifts of all persons. He welcomes and accepts everyone.

*For more information or
to schedule an appointment:*
Phone: (519) 433-0981
Email: btallman@rogers.com
website: www.brucetallman.com
Office: 163 Britannia Avenue, London, Ontario, N6H 2J6

Feel free to forward this email brochure to others who you think might be interested. Your family members, relatives, friends, and co-workers are most welcome.

Approach Churches And Synagogues

You can also contact priests, pastors, ministers, and rabbis about the possibility of you coming to their church or synagogue and doing spiritual direction there one morning, afternoon, or evening once a week or once a month. Let these religious leaders know that anyone who came to see you would pay you directly. Thus, it costs the church or synagogue nothing and it is another service they provide that can be advertised in their bulletin.

One church allowed me to use their comfortable and quiet reconciliation room. Another church let me use their old photocopying room. It was private on Mondays when no one was around, but the chairs were uncomfortable so I brought my own fold-up chairs from home. For some churches, their insurance policy will only let you be in the building when church staff are around, so you may have to inquire at several churches before you find suitable conditions. Again, it is providential and circumstantial.

Retreat Centers

Often, people go away for a retreat and after they experience spiritual direction on the retreat, they want to find a spiritual director in their own city. If you get to know the spiritual direction staff at retreat centers within a two hour driving radius of where you live, they might refer people to you who come to the retreat center from your city.

The "Seek and Find" Guide

Spiritual Directors International (SDI) has developed a "Seek and Find" service on their website at www.sdiworld.org. For a modest fee, members of SDI can post a one hundred word message about their services on the Seek and Find Guide. If you are a member but don't want to pay the fee, SDI will just post your name and contact information.

Anyone anywhere in the world who is seeking a spiritual director thus has access to a whole list of spiritual directors, and can usually find one in their local area. I chose to pay the fee, and within a month someone contacted me and we began spiritual direction. Paying the fee is definitely worth it as the client's payment to you will quickly make up for it. Also, since SDI is the major spiritual direction organization in the world, they make sure that when someone types "spiritual direction" or "spiritual director" into a search engine like Google, SDI comes up on the first page of the million or so websites found. This is important, because the average spiritual director does not have the cumulative power of SDI. Your own website might come up on page ten.

Free Consultations

If someone expresses interest in what you are doing, you could offer them a free one hour consultation in your office. In the consultation ask a few key questions such as "Why are you interested in spiritual direction or counseling?"or "What do you want to work on in your spiritual life?" Then let them do most of the talking while you try to discern their main spiritual need.

After they have talked for a while, state the needs you see; for example, " It sounds like your main need is to have a better prayer life" or "You sound stressed out. I'd like to help you develop trust more, so you are more at peace." Then suggest the steps you could take together to meet that need. Go over your services briefly and then, if you both want to continue, set up the next meeting. If they are not sure they want to continue, give them a copy of your brochure to take with them and suggest they pray about it and call you if they have questions or want to set up an appointment. Then pray about it and wait for about a week.

I usually phone people back in a week if I haven't heard from them, just to see where they are at. Often they were thinking of calling me to set up an appointment, they just hadn't gotten around to it. The longer they leave it, the less likely they are to call me, so I take the initiative and call them. They usually thank me for nudging them to actually set up an appointment.

If they are not interested in doing spiritual direction or counseling, I thank them for meeting with me, let them know my door is always open in case they change their mind, ask if it is okay if I phone them again in three months, and wish them well.

If it is more convenient, the consultation could be done by phone, and you could mail or email your brochure to them. However, it is usually better if they come to see you in person so that they know that spiritual direction will be done in a comfortable setting and you can take note of their body language.

Being Up Front About Openings

If you don't tell them you have openings, people may just assume that you are full up with clients, and therefore never refer people to you, or ask for an appointment for themselves. This is always a little delicate though. If you say you have lots of openings they may wonder why and draw the conclusion that you are not very good at what you do.

The safest thing to say is "I have a few openings in my practice right now that I am looking to fill." Include this whenever you are explaining to people what you do. This lets people know you are receptive to new directees without making you sound desperate for them, which conveys a negative message.

CHAPTER FOUR

Finding Seekers Through Talks, Workshops, and Retreats

Basic Principles

A basic principle for getting hired in any line of work is: it's not only what you know but also who you know, and who knows you, that gets you hired. The most important consequence of giving talks, workshops, and retreats is that it raises awareness of you so that people get to know you and that they can trust you. Those who trust you will either come to you for spiritual guidance or refer others to you. Referrals follow the service you give in presentations.

A second basic principle is to develop talks, workshops, and retreats that can be repeated. Each of us has only so much life energy with which to do our work, and constantly developing new presentations is very time consuming. If you want to attract a lot of seekers, you cannot spend a major portion of your time on presentation development, unless you charge exorbitant fees for the actual presentation, which will make fewer organizations able to afford you. If you want to have time for other important things (such as actually doing spiritual counseling with paying seekers), you would be well-advised to use the same presentation more than once. You will have to change the name of the talk, as well as adapt and update your repeatable presentation somewhat to each new situation, so it will not be identical each time anyway.

A third basic principle for generating referrals from public speaking is to speak your basic message *with enthusiasm*. It is not only the content but the manner of delivery that is important. Groups such as Toastmasters International can help you learn effective public speaking, but the general rule is: don't pick topics you don't care about. Don't just speak about what you think *they* want to hear, also speak about what *you* are passionate about, because what people want to hear are passionate speakers. Any topic can be fascinating if the speaker is excited about it. So, speak about topics that are of vital interest to you.

Benefits of Doing Presentations

Giving talks, workshops, and retreats can be a major source of recruiting new seekers, of income, of variety in your work, and of fun and laughter for you.

Intensely listening to people day after day is hard work, and seekers inevitably share their struggles and problems, so it is normal for a spiritual director or counselor to absorb a certain amount of negativity from their clients.

A great way to shake off this negativity is to get together with a group of adults for some mutual purpose such as a workshop. Usually, if any of them has a sense of humor, a lot of laughter ensues, the endorphins start flowing, and everyone enjoys the time together. When spiritually-oriented adults meet, Spirit is particularly present, joy happens, and our spiritual direction work becomes a living, group thing.

Nothing gains peoples' trust more than actually meeting you face-to-face and getting a sense of who you are and what you are about. Communications experts say we give off hundreds of non-verbal messages by the way we dress, groom ourselves, and behave. If your verbal and nonverbal messages say the same thing—that you are competent, approachable, and caring, people will be attracted to doing spiritual counseling with you.

Some spiritual directors (usually the extroverts!) enjoy giving presentations so much that work with groups becomes a greater source of income than spiritual direction with individuals. Some like to just give the occasional talk, workshop, or retreat as a source of variety in their work, or to get out of their house or office and into the community.

There are a number of other bonuses that can happen when you give presentations. First of all, some of the people at your presentation may invite you to give a presentation to groups they belong to. That group or organization may then advertise you in their newsletter or their church's bulletin as a guest presenter.

Spending money on your own mail-outs and advertising is time consuming and expensive, but being advertised by a group costs you nothing, raises your credibility and perceived trustworthiness immensely (again people trust what others say about you more than they trust what you say about you), and gets your name out to people who you would have no means of contacting otherwise. Those who attend your presentation will inevitably tell others how it went, and so word-of-mouth will spread your name far and wide.

I approached the director of a retreat center about giving a retreat there, he agreed, and they included a description of my retreat in their bi-annual mailing. So, my name got out to about four thousand people twice in one year, people who otherwise I would have no connection with. One of them was a pastoral minister who couldn't attend the retreat, but she invited me to give a similar presentation at her church.

If I had direct-mailed all those people it would have cost me about $2500 in postage each time and untold hours of envelope stuffing and probably would have generated few results. People feel safe if someone is sponsored by an institution they know and trust. On my own, I would have just been a flier in the mail from some unknown person, something to be glanced at and then filed under "garbage."

Lining Up Talks, Workshops, and Retreats

The first step is to list all the topics you could give talks, workshops, and retreats on *with authority and enthusiasm.* It won't work if you try to give presentations on subjects you know little about and for which you have no passion. Here is a list of some of the presentations I give, which may spark your memory of what you have done in the past, or fuel your imagination about what you could do in the future:

Talks

What is Wisdom? Gives the seven characteristics of wisdom according to the Wisdom books in the scriptures. Crucial for our high-tech information age that floods us with knowledge but not wisdom. Our consumer society needs to rediscover why "Wisdom is more precious than gold."

What is Truth? Religions get into conflict over their conflicting truth claims. The "degrees of truth" approach is the only one that allows you to be faithful to *your* truth while at the same time being open to the truth of *others*. It allows both religious commitment and religious tolerance.

What is an Adult Faith? Outlines the ten characteristics of a mature Christian faith based on the reflections of a Harvard professor and a Catholic archbishop.

What is Spiritual Direction? An overview of what spiritual direction is, and how it differs from psychological counseling, pastoral counseling, confessional counseling, and New Age counseling.

The Riches of Scripture. The Word of God can enrich our spiritual lives more than anything else. Teaches a well-balanced approach to scripture and effective methods for getting into it.

Prayer of the Heart. Sometimes called Christian meditation or centering prayer, prayer of the heart has an extensive history, from the Desert Fathers and Mothers to modern masters like John Main. It is a way to "Be still and know that I am God."

Ways of Discerning God's Will. Numerous methods to follow and questions to ask as you try to discern what God wants you to do. Uses Ignatius of Loyola's "discernment of spirits" as a guide.

God, the Center of Evolution. The theory of evolution has had a greater impact on the modern world view than anything else. Scientists are very certain that, contrary to "creationism", things *do* evolve. A different religious view of evolution, that of Teilhard de Chardin, is that all of nature is being guided by God toward the Reign of God on earth. This talk outlines how this is so, and honors both the Christian and scientific world views.

Inner Peace for an Age of Stress. Thirty-one principles for finding God-centered peace of mind in our stressed-out world. Stress is the underlying cause of almost all our problems and illnesses.

Practicing one of these principles a day will help anyone suffering from stress.

Sacred Sexuality. It is possible to find God through holy sexuality. Sexuality as a way to God. Attitudes, values, and God's rules for truly fulfilling sexuality.

The Enneagram: Discerning Your Spiritual Gifts. The Enneagram is a powerful tool used widely in spiritual direction and retreat centers that helps you discover your main spiritual strengths and weaknesses, resulting in greater self-understanding and spiritual growth.

On God and Suffering. A Christian response to the atheist's question: if there is a loving God why is there so much suffering in the world?

Twelve Ways God Loves You. People often say they would like to know God's love more. This talk describes all the ways God loves us.

Workshops

Praying with the Myers Briggs Type Indicator. The MBTI is a personality inventory with a wide variety of applications and uses. Depending on which of the sixteen Myers Briggs types you are, certain types of prayer and certain spiritual paths may feel natural or be hard for you. This workshop helps you discover your Myers Briggs type and new ways to pray and seek God.

Family Understanding Through the Myers Briggs. Knowing what type you, your spouse, and your children are can go a long way to helping you understand each other, and how to get along better. Knowing why people do what they do leads to self-acceptance and acceptance of others.

Lectio Divina. Lectio Divina, done in a group, is both fun and serious. You will be amazed at the spiritual insights that happen as you reflect as a group on sacred scripture. You can also use this method of scripture study for private reflection by yourself in the comfort of your home.

Spiritual Direction Workshop. Same as in the talk above "What is Spiritual Direction?" We will also discuss the many types of issues that come up in spiritual direction and do some group spiritual direction.

The Enneagram Workshop. Same as in the talk above "The Enneagram." After the talk we will use a questionnaire and readings as well as feedback from the facilitator and others to discover our actual Enneagram type. Books on the Enneagram are also discussed.

Developing a Spiritual Mission and Goals for Your Life. If you know what God is calling you to, what your spiritual mission and goals are, you can orient your whole life around these things. This has a big impact because it gives participants a real sense of purpose and direction for their life.

Christianity and Self-Esteem. Selfishness is not healthy, but loving ourselves in a healthy way is the essence of mental health, moral living, happiness, and one of the Great Commandments of Christ. Come and find out how you can build your self-esteem in a Christian way.

Finding God at Home and Work. This workshop focuses on the signs of God that are all around us. All we need to do is wake up to them. We can find God in the wonders of creation, human relationships, sexuality, work, and play.

Christian Time Management. Jesus said "Put God first, and everything else will be taken care of." This workshop gives you a practical way to combine the best time management skills with Christian values. Helps you learn to make God and God's ways a priority in your life.

Archetypes and Spiritual Growth. Archetypes form the basic structure of the male and female soul and affect everything we do. We will learn how we can grow spiritually by activating the four heroic archetypes of Sovereign, Warrior, Seer, and Lover, and by avoiding the anti-heroic archetypes of Tyrant, Abdicator, Sadist, Masochist, Manipulator, Fool, Addict, and Frigid.

Inner Peace Principles. An interactive workshop based on the talk of the same name above.

Prayer Sampler Workshop. We will sample four different types of prayer: Lectio Divina, Ignatian Prayer, Centering Prayer, and Taize Prayer.

Family Spirituality. Focuses on the importance of the family as the church at home, the domestic church, and gives principles for happiness in marriage and parenting.

Finding Seekers: Recruitment Methods for Developing a Spiritual Direction Practice. A professional development workshop for spiritual directors or interns. Half-day or full-day formats.

The Couple Communication Method. Teaches married couples how to communicate well and safely resolve conflict. Involves hands-on practice of the method by the couples at the workshop.

Retreats

Introduction to Spiritual Direction/Re-orienting Your Life. Where have you come from, and where are you going to spiritually? By writing your Spiritual Autobiography and Spiritual Mission Statement, and by two sessions of spiritual guidance with a professional spiritual director, this retreat will help you re-orient your life. Lots of group work and time for individual reflection and prayer. Also includes an introduction to the Enneagram which can help you discover your spiritual strengths and weaknesses.

Archetypal Christian Living. The archetypes of Sovereign, Warrior, Seer, and Lover form the basic structure of every man and woman's soul. These inner heroes help us overcome the Shadow archetypes: the Tyrant, Abdicator, Sadist, Masochist, Manipulator, Fool, Addict, and Frigid that subconsciously destroy us. This retreat focuses on identifying the positive and negative archetypes operating in us, and on activating our inner heroes for empowered Christian living. Retreatants will also be introduced to the archetypes of the Enneagram, and have an opportunity to explore all this in spiritual direction.

Warriors of the Heart. Men's work with a Christian spirituality focus. We will experience dying to the "old man," the false ideas of masculinity handed to men by our culture, and we will put on the "new man" modeled by Jesus, with an emphasis also on Jungian models of authentic, healthy manhood. Done in a context of prayer, small group work, individual solitude, and a community of Christian men. Facilitated by Bruce Tallman and Patrick O'Connor.

Empowered Spirituality Retreat. Take your spiritual journey to the next level. *Friday night:* We will learn our Myers-Briggs personality types and numerous forms of prayer and meditation that work for the different types, as well as practice Centering Prayer.

Saturday morning: We will practice new ways of approaching sacred scripture: Lectio Divina and Ignatian Prayer. *Saturday afternoon:* The Enneagram will help us understand our main spiritual strengths (joy, wisdom, compassion, etc) and areas needing spiritual growth (pride, greed, envy, etc). *Saturday night:* Archetypes will help us understand the structure of the human soul, both when it is healthy (the positive archetypes of Sovereign/Leader, Warrior/Prophet, Seer/Wise One, and Lover/Contemplative) and not-so-healthy (the negative archetypes of Tyrant/Abdicator, Sadist/Masochist, Manipulator/Fool, Addict/Frigid). *Sunday morning:* We will each develop a Spiritual Mission Statement which can be used for lifelong spiritual guidance and a Spiritual Rule which will give us daily spiritual habits to practice. On Sunday morning there will also be time for Mass, Protestant services, or a meditation service, depending on what participants want.

Testimonies About the Empowered Spirituality Retreat: "Vitally helpful for increasing the health of one's spiritual life. Enlightening, accessible, and practical help for prayer and spiritual growth." — *Rev. Phil Newman, Riverside United Church*; "Excellent, calming and easy-to-follow. A wonderful spiritual journey into my soul." — *Lucy Uptgrove, Church of St. Jude (Anglican)*; "An amazing journey of looking at my true self. I really got a sense of who I am and where I am on my spiritual journey. The various ways to pray and connect to God were wonderful and welcomed spiritual food." —*Sherry Gabison, Registered Nurse*; "A safe, nonjudgmental, informative atmosphere and a realistic approach to spirituality created by a knowledgeable and easy-to-understand facilitator." —*John Langford, Retired Doctor*

Secondly, list all the possible groups you could give your presentations to. Here are some possibilities:

Presentation Contacts

Retreat Centers: see Spiritual Directors International list: www.sdiworld.org/retreat_centers.html

Hospital/University/College/School Chaplains Gatherings
Libraries: talk on the spirituality of topics of wide public interest
University and College Continuing Education Departments
Religious Schools: contact the Religious Education Department
Hospitals: speak on spirituality and health
Seniors Groups: speak on spirituality and aging
Anti-Addiction Groups (AA, EA, GA, OA, SA, etc.): speak on spirituality and addiction
Internal Church Organizations: Clergy Gatherings/Women's Groups/Men's Groups/Marriage Preparation/Married Couples Groups/Prayer Groups/Bible Study Groups
Church Committees: Liturgy/Social Justice/Youth/Bereavement/Seniors
External Church Organizations: Cursillo/St. Vincent de Paul/Alpha
Service Clubs: Lions, Rotary, Kiwanis, etc: speak on spirituality and service
Businesses: speak on spirituality and work or spiritual health for employees

The biggest barrier to people getting to know you is the cost of your presentations. If you charge too much, organizations may not take you on as a presenter. On the other hand, if you don't charge a reasonable fee, they may not respect you or they may treat you with suspicion. Therefore, you need to discern what is appropriate for each organization you approach. Nobody wants to go to a free talk that is just a boring lecture about your work, so if you are giving a free talk make sure it has an emotional impact on your listeners, and gives them value. You may find it easier to get sponsored by a church if your talk is free, because churches favor presentations that don't create financial barriers for the poor. If you don't want to just give a free talk, consider giving a free lecture on Friday night followed by a paid full-day workshop on Saturday. Businesses and other organizations will expect you to charge a fee.

A creative way of doing ongoing presentations would be to give a free two hour session in your office once a month in which you teach the participants a new way of prayer each time: Taize prayer, lectio divina, centering prayer, Ignatian prayer and so on. Email all your present and former clients and ask them to invite their family and friends, who can also forward the email to people they know.

Here is a possible format:

- start with a brief prayer and check-in where people give their name and say a little about how they pray.
- give a five or ten minute engaging talk about spiritual direction
- explain the type of prayer for that night and have them do it
- ask them to share how that prayer experience was for them
- build on their comments and explain that this is the kind of thing they would learn in spiritual direction
- wrap up with a closing prayer

This can be a very effective way of recruiting seekers because they learn your location, get to see your office, learn about spiritual direction, and experience the benefits of a new way of praying. This experience will have more impact on them than mere words and graphics on a brochure or web site, and most importantly, they get to meet, know, and trust *you*. All you have to do on your part is detach from the results and do the session for the fun of it, as something you are doing "pro bono" because you enjoy helping others grow spiritually. That's why you got into this in the first place, right?

You could also develop a one or two page email résumé listing all your talks, workshops, and retreats. Then phone churches, synagogues, and organizations listed in the Yellow Pages, explain who you are and that you give presentations to groups, and ask if you emailed them your list of talks, workshops, and retreats would they pass the list on to groups within the organization that might be interested? Or you could ask the church or organization secretary for the name and email or phone number of the contact person and then phone or email them to ask if you can send them your list of presentations.

Or use the Yellow Pages to find out the names of churches and organizations and then Google these names to see if they have a website. Sometimes websites list groups within the organization and even list the email of the group leaders. You could then email your list of presentations directly to that person with an appropriate cover letter.

In order to keep track of who you emailed and what you said in the emails, it helps to keep a "Presentations" file box. List on the file cards the group's name and the name, phone number, and email of the contact person, as well as what you sent them and when. Then just keep prioritizing your cards according to the likelihood of a favorable response. Beyond phoning and emailing people (or email-ing first and then phoning), it would be good to visit them and build your relationship with them.

There is client contact/client relations management software out there that businesses use to keep track of their customers that could be more effective than mere index cards, but then it has to be bought and downloaded, and you have to learn how to use it. Some of the software would come with tutorials, but if you prefer to be low-tech, file cards will do nicely.

You could also host a gathering of therapists, psychologists, social workers, and other spiritual counselors and explain what you do. Meeting you will increase their trust of you, and subsequently, their referrals to you.

How To Give Presentations

When you are doing a presentation, it is important to relax and build a relationship with your audience. Don't just give facts, make it experiential. You could start with a human interest story about common spiritual trials and temptations. Nothing grips the listener's imagination like story-telling. Then ask them questions to get them thinking and talking. Make it participatory and fun for everyone.

Outline where they might be now on their spiritual journey, and where spiritual counseling could take them. Be sure to mention all the benefits of spiritual counseling and how it could help them with all their spiritual struggles.

You could get them to talk about the confusion, busyness, and despair of modern life and then have them do centering prayer or a simple meditation on the Higher Power's care and providence, so they can experience a solution to the problem. The main thing is to make your presentations engaging. Here are some guidelines for doing presentations:

Presentation Guidelines

1. Be specific in your topic. E.g.: not "How to Grow Spiritually" but "How to Do Prayer of the Heart."
2. Pick topics with wide interest so you get as many people as possible.
3. Consider doing it free of charge or for "donations only" (you benefit from their advertising you, getting to know you, and you getting to know them).
4. Make eye contact with your audience—don't read your presentation.
5. Engage in self-disclosure: let them know you are human.
6. Use stories.
7. Use humor, but don't force or plan it. Let it flow spontaneously out of you and your topic.
8. Use everyday examples people can relate to.
9. Talk extemporaneously from an outline. You may have to practice this at home.
10. Read audience body language for signs of boredom, tension, etc. Ask questions every now and then to keep them involved.
11. Be animated without overdoing it.
12. Give handouts.
13. Use A/V aids, particularly PowerPoint.
14. Include individual reflection, small group, and large group work.

It's important to have your audience evaluate your presentation, and on your Workshop Evaluation Form invite them to give their name, email, phone number, organization they work for, position within that organization, and ask if you can quote them. This can help you in three ways. You can contact workshop participants later to ask them if they are interested in giving spiritual direction a try. You can also email them about other workshops you are doing. As well, it can be a source of positive testimonies about the workshop when you promote the workshop in the future. Here is the form I use for this:

Workshop Evaluation Form

1. What was helpful to you in this workshop?

2. What was not helpful to you in this workshop?

3. How could this workshop be improved?

4. How would you describe this workshop and the facilitator to someone else?

5. Permission to quote the above: yes_____ no_____

Please Print:

Name_____

Phone_____

Email:_____

Position &
Organization_____

CHAPTER FIVE

Finding Seekers Through Networking

Becoming a spiritual counselor is all about practice promotion—that is, systematically and ethically conveying the message first of all, that you are out there, and secondly, you are competent and professional.

The best way to do this is through networking. However, what is "networking"? "Networking" was always a puzzling buzz word for me until I finally realized that it just means "getting out there and meeting people in key positions who you can help and who can help you."

At one point I was contemplating taking some courses with a college in Toronto that trains spiritual counselors. Knowing that it would be expensive, I asked the registrar if I could talk to some of the graduates to see how they were doing. I was surprised to learn that, after spending fifteen thousand dollars for a two year full-time program, only one out of the thirty people I talked to was actually working full-time in the field she had studied. Everyone I phoned agreed that this one person was successful because she networked.

There are many reasons why people don't get out and meet other professionals—that is, network. Here are some of them:

- shyness
- feeling I have nothing to offer
- belief that one should be well-established in one's practice before networking
- fear that the other person will find out I am not a professional
- not knowing how to go about networking
- not believing that networking is important
- no time to do it, a full-time job or day classes prevent it
- not knowing who to network with

Learning how to network can help us overcome the fears that are the biggest block to getting out there.

Basic Principles Of Networking

First of all, remember the dictum "Referrals follow service." What most other professionals want to know is: how can *you* serve *them*? They are not interested in how they can serve you. They don't care that you don't have many clients yet, so don't ask them *directly* for referrals. Simply build a relationship with them.

To build relationships with professionals you don't know, there is a sequence of steps to go through. Keep in mind that it is a good idea anyway to know the therapists, psychologists, social workers, and other professionals in your area so you could refer directees to them if they need the kind of help these people offer. So, first send these people a letter or email expressing interest in finding out more about their services, since you may want to refer your clients to them. The other steps are to call the professional, set up a meeting, have the meeting, and then send them a follow-up letter thanking them for the meeting. In this final letter include your brochure. It's better here to use snail mail than email so you know they have received an actual copy of your brochure. If you send them an email brochure, they may never open it.

To refer people to you, professionals first of all need to know who you are, what you do, and that you are trained, skilled, and qualified in what you do. They also need to know how you are different from other spiritual counselors such as priests, ministers, or pastoral counselors.

During the course of meeting them, all of this will probably come up. If you are interested in their services, they will probably express interest in what you do. So, go into the meeting prepared to ask intelligent questions about what they do (you may need to do some research on them beforehand), clearly convey what you do, when you are available, and how your services are unique. If they have clients who have religious or spiritual concerns, or want to speak to someone trained in spirituality, or who want to speak to a counselor from their own faith, the professionals you visit may refer their clients to you.

The basic message you want to convey is *you*. Therefore you want others to hear about *you* and from *you* as much as possible. It takes usually four contacts with *you* for a professional to make *you* a permanent part of his or her memory banks. Therefore, following the four steps of the initial letter or email, phone call, visit, and follow-up thank you letter accomplishes this.

All four steps are important, but always remember that face time (visiting) is far more important than voice time (phoning) and voice time is always far more effective than paper time (letter or email writing). For example, when I was working for the Diocese of London, Ontario a fellow came all the way from Windsor (about a ninety minute drive) to explain his services to me. This disposed me to using his services far more than if I had just received his résumé or brochure in the mail. Résumés, employment experts tell us, usually receive about a ten second glance before an employer files them away (often in the round file).

Although visiting may seem excessively time-consuming in the short run, in the long run it is much more efficient and time-saving because it produces far greater results (clients) than the other three steps. But it takes courage to visit people—that's why keeping in mind that you are visiting them to find out what *they* do is so important—it takes all the pressure off of you. You don't have to perform, you just have to be interested in them. And, of course, like most people, they will love to talk about what *they* do.

To locate professionals who are relevant to the field of spiritual counseling, one of the best resources is church directories or web sites. You can usually find the head office of any diocese or denomination in your local area in your phone book or on the Internet under "churches." Their web site may list all the contact people you need, but if it doesn't, call them up and ask them if they sell a directory to the public. In my diocese, the chancery (head) office sells a directory that lists all Southwestern Ontario Catholic parishes, educational institutions, health care services, social service agencies, priests, lay ministers, principals, chaplains, psychologists, social workers, retreat centers, and all their contact information. Anyone can buy the directory for a few dollars. The local Anglican (Episcopalian) diocese lists all of this on their web site.

In most urban areas there are usually local directories or magazines of all the alternate health care services. Besides listing things like various types of massage, Reiki, hypnotherapy, channeling angels, and so on, they usually include various schools of spiritual teaching and practice. You may be able to find contacts here for places where you could give spiritual workshops or do spiritual counseling.

In most areas there are also directories of Christian businesses and services. For example *The Shepherd's Guide* lists every businessperson in London who considers him or herself to be a Christian from a wide range of fields: dentists, chiropractors, counselors, office suppliers, photographers, real estate agents, and so on. It also lists every church of every denomination, as well as every Christian campground, conference center, radio station, head office, book store, food bank, thrift store, mission, music ministry, prayer network, resource center, social support agency, and youth ministry in the greater London area. Since these types of directories are supported by their advertisers they are provided free of charge to the general public and are usually distributed to every church in the area. Check the brochure racks at the back of churches or ask priests or ministers if he or she has heard of such a resource in your area. Or go online and Google "The Shepherd's Guide+(your city)" and see if anything comes up. These directories can be a goldmine of contact information for the fledgling spiritual director.

You will also want to maintain a "Network Contacts" file box similar to the one you have for presentations. Again, you could use software for this, but 3 inch by 5 inch cards and a plastic box to hold them (which you can get at any office supply store) can work well. Keep a record of what happened in every contact you made as well as all of the person's contact information. Keep prioritizing all of this on a regular basis in terms of where you believe you will receive the most fruitful response.

You can network from the top down or from the bottom up, and both approaches have their advantages. You could start at the top of an organization's structure, for example, with the bishop, and then work your way down. If you get the approval of the upper levels of management, it can carry a lot of weight with those on the lower levels. If you can go to a priest and say you have the bishop's approval, it can smooth the way and open a lot of doors. On the other hand, if you go to the bishop and he rejects you and sends an email to all the priests not to meet with you, you could be finished all the way from the top to the bottom

Those at the top of an organization are often surprisingly approachable, but if starting off with the upper ranks of an organization is too intimidating for you, or if it would take too long to get an appointment, then consider working from the bottom up. If you wanted to approach a particular priest, you might start by approaching the leader of some group in the parish, or one of the parish staff, get that person on your side, and then ask that person to approach the priest for you. If the priest knows you well, you could approach him directly, but if he doesn't know you, his staff or other parish leaders would carry more weight with him or her than you would.

In this regard, never underestimate the power of the secretaries of any organization. A cartoon showed a sign on a secretary's desk that said "Do you want to talk to the boss or to someone who knows what's going on around here?" Secretaries are a potential major source of referrals. They are the first person the public talks to when they call the organization, they are the gatekeepers of the organization. Indeed, they may have a better understanding of what is currently happening in an organization and be more knowledgeable of who is currently doing what than the leaders, simply because almost everyone goes through the secretary to connect with everyone else, or relies upon her or him for knowledge of resources.

So, it is important to treat secretaries well. Don't brush them off when you phone the organization, take time to talk to them, get to know them, and help them get to know you. Build a relationship with them. In a parish the secretary may refer people directly to counselors because they don't want to bother the priest. I get a lot of referrals that way.

Every client who comes to see you brings with him or her a network of people, groups, agencies, clubs, churches, and schools with which they are connected. Therefore, another way of working from the bottom up is to ask your client, when you fill out an "intake form" at the first session with them, about any groups they belong to. Several sessions later, before or after the spiritual counseling session, in person or by email, you could ask the client who would be a good person to network with in each group. Then contact and network with these people. Use your own discretion as to when it would be appropriate or not appropriate to ask clients for this information.

If a client wants to connect to a priest, minister, or church, you could make some recommendations if you know the local clergy. You could also call that priest or minister and let them know that you are referring someone to their church. This usually makes clergy very happy. Or, if you need to refer someone to a therapist, you could get involved with the referral and phone the therapist (with the client's permission) to let them know you are referring someone so that the therapist gets to know you as well as the new client.

After a few sessions, if you think it would be appropriate and the client would agree, you could also ask the client for permission to contact their priest, minister, pastor, or therapist in order to let these professionals know you are doing spiritual direction with one of their people. You would be doing this just as a professional courtesy, not disclosing to them anything that is transpiring between you and your client.

If you do contact these professionals, make sure you let them know that the client gave you permission to do this. This will help these other professionals realize that you are out there and that you have an impact on their people. It also makes you accountable, in some ways, to these professionals. They may ask your client how the spiritual direction sessions with you are going. Respecting your client's boundaries is always of paramount importance, so again, use your discretion about if, when, and how to proceed with this.

Teaming Up With Other Professionals to Help People

Ministers, priests, or rabbis with big congregations often feel overwhelmed. They don't have time to see everyone for individual counseling and therefore might welcome a spiritual director or counselor who they can trust as someone to refer people to. If there are local clergy associations or get-togethers that have guest speakers at their meetings, try to get on the agenda for five minutes or more in which you briefly explain your services. This way you would be addressing a bunch of clergy at the same time, a very efficient way to do things.

As I wrote earlier, don't be afraid to work ecumenically. Although spiritual direction was previously thought of as something that emerged from the Catholic church, more and more Christian and non-Christian groups are embracing it. Mennonites, Presbyterians, Anglicans (Episcopalians), Jews, Buddhists, and many others have rapidly adopted it.

Chaplains at hospitals and universities can also be a good source of referrals. Hospital chaplains often have patients of no religious or denominational affiliation, or who have an affiliation but are not attending services of their religion or denomination, but who would be ready to explore the spiritual dimension of their illness when they return home. If a person has passed away, their friends and relatives might be open to exploring their thoughts and feelings in spiritual counseling. University students in seminaries often are required to have a spiritual director.

If priests, ministers, rabbis, and chaplains know you work evenings and weekends they may be glad to refer people to you who can only meet during the off-hours. For many priests and ministers, Mondays are part of their off-hours.

You could work with therapists, psychotherapists, psychologists, psychiatrists, and social workers of every kind as a teacher or consultant in cases where their clients' problems are based in their religious beliefs or upbringing. Or the therapist could refer the client directly to you. You could also work with the staff of emergency hotlines preparing them for people whose spiritual or religious beliefs are part of the crisis. For example, a person phoning in might believe that God has abandoned them, or that their life is meaningless and hopeless, or they are going to hell.

Every spiritual counselor will benefit from joining Spiritual Directors International, attending their annual conference if possible, and using their directory to locate and network with other spiritual counselors who live in their local area. Or there might already exist a local association of spiritual counselors (such as Spiritual Directors of Ontario) that has an online or printed newsletter, regular meetings, and their own annual conference. These organizations can be a gateway to many rewarding contacts. If you know spiritual counselors in several cities, and they know you, you can refer clients to each other if those clients are transferred or decide to move.

If you know spiritual directors in your local area who have lots of clients, invite them to coffee or lunch and find out what they do and how they do it. Let them get to know you and that you are available if they have an overflow or they find that they and some of their clients are not well-matched.

You have to be a bit cautious in all of the above cases though, that therapists, social workers, chaplains, ministers, and other spiritual counselors do not just send you their most problematic cases. Suggest that any new clients try a few sessions with you so you can both discern whether or not it is a good fit. Naturally, you need to pray a lot and discern well in all of this. Perhaps some "problematic cases" are just people who have a fear of being rejected by others, and your unconditional love of them can help them get past this.

Spiritual directors who work at colleges, seminaries, or retreat houses have a distinct advantage. Since they work for an institution, it is easier for them to become known and trusted, so they often get many more referrals than the person in private practice. However, as with chaplains and others, they might refer people to you who can only meet in the off-hours.

You could also team up with the staff of church marriage tribunals, or with spiritually-oriented lawyers or financial planners. These people often work with people in family break-ups. Spouses, children, and relatives of the couple who are breaking up might feel a need for some spiritual guidance.

CHAPTER SIX

Finding Seekers Through Advertising

Brochures

The best way to figure out how to do a brochure is to consider what people do *not* want in a brochure. If you want to turn people off, here are some key ingredients:

- an uninteresting cover
- technical or clinical language (eg. "Nineteenth Annotation")
- make it hard to read (too much text, not enough blank space)
- have a negative tone (dwell on problems, not benefits)
- sound impersonal, dogmatic, and institutional

Before you begin you should ponder what various types of words, paper, fonts, design, logos, colors, symbols, and photos convey about your practice? Do they say your practice is successful, professional, enjoyable, old-fashioned, progressive, closed-minded?

Here are some guidelines for a well-made brochure:

Brochure Guidelines

- define your target audience, that is, who you want to reach
- define one single objective for your brochure: what do you want them to do after they read it?

- define the impression you want to make: scholarly? friendly? best in field? different? traditional?
- define a clear single benefit they will get from your services
- create credibility (without exaggerating) with A. convincers like "In our fifteen years of experience we have found that..."; B. what your service limits are... "spiritual direction is not therapy"; C. your professional credentials and affiliations
- use plain English
- make the brochure worth keeping. E.g.: include "Ten Principles For..."
- put a 'people picture' on the cover
- print on quality color stock
- tell a story
- have an effective title: either A. ask a question. Eg: "Spiritual Direction?"or B. enumerate means to an end. Eg: "Seven Steps to Discern God's Will" or "How to..."
- section headings within the brochure should be in question form. Eg: "How does Spiritual Guidance Work?" "Who is the Spiritual Director?"
- make it easy to read: as few words and as much blank space as possible. The shorter, the more likely it will be read.
- gently suggest an action you want them to take: "Please call..."

Once you have your brochure done, ask a few people who you trust to give you some honest feedback on it, and make any changes you deem to be reasonable before printing large quantities of it.

You could use the information on your brochure as content for your website. In fact, the proper order in which to proceed is this: first design a prototype of your brochure. Then take the information from your brochure and give it to someone who can design for you a nice one to three page website. Once the website is designed you can put your website's Internet address on your brochure and then get a bunch of them printed off.

If you don't do things in this order, you will end up with hundreds of brochures which are missing an essential ingredient, that is, your website address. On the other hand, you could get your brochures printed right away, so you can quickly get them out there, then work on your website, and then include your website address on your second batch of brochures.

Spiritual Directors International has designed some glossy, professional-looking, low-cost brochures that any spiritual director could use (see https://secure.sdiworld.org/zencart/). The more you order, the lower the cost per brochure. Although rather generic in nature, they have left spaces on these brochures where you can attach your business card or stamp them so that people get your specific contact information.

Again, ask permission before you put your brochures out in laundromats, waiting rooms, bookstores and so on. Churches (and probably synagogues and mosques) have rules about who can affix things to their notice boards and use their brochure racks.

Newsletters

You could email a monthly, bimonthly, or quarterly newsletter, but it must be of value to the recipients. In other words, people don't want to receive just advertising. I receive a monthly email from someone in Australia and it is all about them and what they are up to, so I never read it.

People also don't like reading long messages on their computer screen, so keep it as brief as possible. Different fonts and images can also make it more interesting.

In your newsletter you could include spiritual quotes, short book reviews, advice on how to grow spiritually, interviews with clients with unusual stories (with their permission), and other "newsy" items. Then give a brief description of your services, and your upcoming talks or workshops.

In addition to, or in place of, emailing a newsletter, you could email any articles you have published, as long as the article is short, no more than eight hundred words. Recipients should be able to read your newsletter or article in three minutes.

I email out a monthly list of "Top Ten Spiritual Growth Ideas" based on the writings of some of the greatest spiritual thinkers of the 20th and 21st centuries. I have condensed each idea so that it is no more than two lines long. I also email out any articles of mine whenever they are published (usually about once a month) in the *London Free Press* "Spirituality and Ethics" section. The articles are only 600 words long.

Forcing yourself to write short articles makes you distill the essence of your thinking. It also increases the chances that what you write will be read. I recommend to the thousand or so people on my email list that they print off the article, and when they have two minutes, give it a quick read. Again, I think spamming is okay as long as it is of value to the reader and not too frequent.

An emailed newsletter or article can be a very cost-effective way of keeping your name fresh in peoples' minds, and it may arrive just when they are ready to give spiritual counseling a try. If it is packed with valuable ideas, they may also forward it to their friends and relatives.

News Releases

Editors need to fill up the allotted space in their periodical or newspaper, and therefore are looking for "fillers" such as news releases. However, to get a news or press release published, it has to be a notice of a free event that would be of interest to as many people as possible rather than just a select few. So, if you are sending in information on a workshop of interest to John and Jane Public, describe the content in a general way, along with dates and contact information. You could also include testimonials from people who have participated in the workshop in the past. A news release is one of the best means of free publicity for your workshops. It can reach a lot of people with little effort on your part.

Here is a sample news/press release:

For Immediate Press Release
A Celebration of World Religions

As a rabbi once said "Every major religion knows how to get us enlightened. What we need now is a way in which we can get enlightened together." The purpose of this day of celebrating world religions is to do just that.

Although every major religion teaches peace, religion has often been a source of conflict and division. This celebration will give representatives of every major religion the chance to share some central prayers and ideas from their tradition on the theme of "world peace", thus creating more harmony and understanding.

The different traditions will also share their food and songs. Everyone is welcome. Refreshments will be served.

What: A Celebration of World Religions
Where: St Peter's Catholic Church, London, Ontario
When: January 15, 2008 from 2:00—4:00pm
Cost: Free
Contact: Bruce Tallman, 519-433-0981,

It could be time-consuming organizing such an event, but as the master of ceremonies, a lot of people will get to know you, and you can recruit people from each religion to help you out with it.

Radio and Television

Every city of one hundred thousand or more people usually has spiritual talk shows on the radio on Sundays. There may even be stations that specialize seven days a week in religion and spirituality. For example, here in London, Ontario (population 350,000) there is Spirit Radio and Grace FM, which are dedicated exclusively to religious programming.

On many television channels there is religious programming on Sunday mornings and, as with radio, some channels specialize in both religion and spirituality. Talk show hosts, whether on radio or television, need guests, so this is an excellent way to promote and explain your services. Hosts might be very interested in having someone explain what this strange new thing called "spiritual direction" is all about, how it differs from psychology and astrology, and so on. You can usually find the website for the radio station or television channel on the Internet, with the email address of the person in charge of programming.

The Cost of Advertising

Promoting your practice through radio, television, YouTube, and other forms of publicity can be free, whereas advertising can be costly. You could get together with other spiritual directors and share the expense of paid advertising. Together you could create a "Spiritual Direction Referral Service" ad that goes into church bulletins, newsletters or even the Yellow Pages of the telephone book, or the spirituality pages of the local newspaper. Advertising once in a while in the spirituality pages will be much less expensive than a permanent ad in the Yellow Pages.

A spiritual direction referral service simply connects people who phone in with spiritual directors who are paying for the ad. People will tend to trust this type of service more than if you advertise individually, although in an individual ad you could include your own website if you have one. In either case, you should emphasize the words "professional" and "affordable."

An ad in a city newspaper for a workshop you are giving might cost you four hundred dollars, but if done effectively, it might also make tens of thousands of people aware of your services. Even if you offered the workshop for free, if even just one or two people want to follow up on the workshop with spiritual counseling, you will quickly regain the cost of the ad and more. One client would just have to come to ten sessions and pay $40 each time for you to recoup your costs, and meanwhile your name will have become known to many people through the ad.

Basic rules for advertising workshops are that you must first get and hold peoples' attention, make your services free or at least affordable for as many people as possible, advertise specific topics, and include your contact information. People are drawn to pictures of a person's face, so include your picture in your ad. The more specific the topic, the better your chances of a response. Specific ads are something people can comprehend or "get a handle on."

Leverage: Getting Others To Advertise For You

"Leverage" means that some other organization, retreat center, or church advertises for you. Your name and workshop title goes to their whole mailing list of thousands of people or goes in their church bulletin for their roster of upcoming events. This, in many ways, is the best publicity of all. First of all, it is free of charge, and secondly, it gives you instant credibility. If an organization, retreat center or church is sponsoring you, you must be good at what you do.

Articles

A well-written article will do more for you than advertising in the Yellow Pages or elsewhere. People read articles far more than ads. Writing articles is an excellent way to get known. People who read your articles will feel like they know you and will come to trust you and your judgment.

For example, I had more response from one "Spiritual Direction Is For Everyone" article in our local diocesan newsletter than I did from fifteen ads in the same paper. The article cost me nothing except several hours of writing and rewriting, whereas the ads cost me $1215.

It is important to remember that editors need articles to fill up the space of their periodical. They need you as much as you need them. They want as many people as possible to read what you have written, so they are looking for human interest stories and what is currently "hot."

There are always new trends emerging in our society, and every trend can be approached from a spiritual angle. For example, the spiritual angle for dieting would be an article on all the spiritual benefits of fasting. You could address your spirituality article to other concerns that millions currently have, such as stress, marital difficulties, the mid-life crisis of baby boomers ("Spiritual Counseling Can Help You Find New Meaning"), aging ("Aging Gracefully Through Spiritual Direction"), retirement, and so on.

What editors are looking for is something "topical," that is, currently relevant to as many people as possible. For example I wrote an article shortly after the first tsunami hit called "How Can God Allow Such Pain?" and another called "How Religions Can Live In Peace" shortly after a particularly bad conflict in the Middle East. Both articles were published in the *London Free Press* which has a distribution of 140,000 readers.

If possible, try to revise and re-use your articles in several different places: local or national periodicals, church newsletters from your denomination or that of others, "zines"(online magazines) and so on. If you get several different articles published in one place, ask the editor if you can do an ongoing column. If you can give regular sound spiritual advice through such a column, you could become the spiritual counselor for an entire town or city, which is what has happened in my case.

Thoughtful articles regularly published should result in a steady flow of clients as well as requests for speaking engagements. My estimate is that I am contacted by one new directee for every article I write, and I am invited to be a speaker a few times a year.

You might be able to become a featured writer every second Saturday or once a month if you feel like a weekly column would be too demanding. Newspapers often pay you for your article. Although it is a small amount, the exposure the article gives you is worth thousands of dollars.

Big-city newspapers in Canada and the United States are usually owned by media conglomerates, and usually have their own writers on contract with them, so it can be next to impossible getting an article published with them. However, in any city there are often many small community or neighborhood newspapers, newsletters, or publications on local holistic health providers that are a lot less formal and are open to contributions from unknown writers.

Books

Nothing will increase your credibility as a spiritual director more than publishing a book. You will find this opens many doors and avenues for you. You can either write a book and send the whole manuscript to a publisher or start off by just sending in a book proposal. Publishers, depending on how well-known they are, might get hundreds of proposals a week, so do not get discouraged by rejection letters.

If you have strong credentials in terms of education, training, and experience, as well as a prior publishing history, (even if it is just articles), and keep sending in very strong book proposals or manuscripts, to a variety of publishers, you should eventually succeed.

Writer's Digest, an annual publication that lists all the publishers and their editors, and has a special section on religion and spirituality, can help you direct your manuscript or proposal to the right place. See www.writersdigest.com.

After the book is published, you should promote the book with frequent speaking engagements. This will give you a proven track record of sales and will show publishers that you will do your share of the work in promoting your book, and make it easier to sell your next book to a major publisher.

You could also self-publish your book. This has several advantages and several drawbacks. First of all, you can avoid the year long wait that regular publishers take to get your book out. Secondly, you control the editing and cover design. Thirdly, you receive all the profits after your initial costs. A regular publisher will give you ten percent of the royalties if they sell it, and forty percent if you sell it. So, if the book sells for $20, you get $2 if they sell it and $8 if you sell it.

On the other hand, if you self-publish, it might cost you $4 per copy to produce the book, but if you sell it for $20, you make a $16 profit. This gives you more incentive to get out there and sell your book in every way possible. A popular way of marketing your book is to give a workshop on your book's topic and include the cost of the book in the workshop cost.

The major advantage of working with a regular publisher is that they take care of the editing, cover design, marketing, advertising, and distribution of the book, which costs you nothing in time, effort, or money. However, while they will give your book a big push at the beginning, they will soon move on to marketing new books, so after about three months from the original publication date, if you don't promote the book yourself it will rapidly be forgotten.

The recognized guru of self-publishing is a man named Dan Poynter. You can access all his tips for free and sign up for his weekly newsletter on self-publishing at his website: http://www.selfpublishing-biz.com/

An original way to do self-publishing, at a fraction of the cost, is being promoted by a company called "Lulu" (see www.lulu.com). They publish individual books as individual orders come in, so that there is no big up front publication costs for say a thousand books, as well as no excess inventory. The Internet has many other websites on the ins and outs of self-publishing.

Websites

It goes without saying that it is important to have your own website in case anyone wants more information about your services. I refer people to my own website (www.brucetallman.com) all the time. Your website should first of all stress the benefits of spiritual direction. You can explain what spiritual direction is, how a typical session works, your particular approach to spiritual direction, and so on. Your website should also include a picture of yourself, a short bio, a list of services you offer, a calendar of upcoming events such as workshops and retreats you are facilitating, and a list of books and articles you have published.

As with newsletters, people don't want your website to be just a big ad for your services. They are often looking for information as well. So you could also include a recommended reading list, links to other websites such as those for SDI or retreat centers, and a link to your monthly newsletter (with a box they can check off if they want to receive it by email every month—this allows you to keep your name before them on a regular basis.) A short description beside each link can also be very helpful for your visitors.

You could ask the owners of the websites that are accessed through links on your site if they would include a link to your site on their website. That way people may come to your site through many other sites.

Also on your website you could include a hit counter on each page and a message that says "You are visitor X since (date)." This allows you to see which pages of your website people are most interested in, and allows you to revise it accordingly. As well, include when your site was last updated, a copyright notice, a pop-up email, and your contact information.

Websites can be costly or simple. Prices for website design can be as little as $500 or as high as $10,000. If you are on a shoe-string budget you might be able to get a high school or college student to design it as part of their course work. Or perhaps you have a friend who is a computer whiz.

Ideally, you could learn how to design a website yourself so that you can change it at will. A good way to find out how to do this is to do an Internet search on "HTMLeditor," "HTML goodies.com," and "HTM.help.com," which include tutorials on web-authoring. You will also have to register your domain name, which is basically your parking spot on the Internet freeway. HostIndex.com or FindMyHosting.com can help you with this. There are also websites that explain how to promote your website on the Internet.

The biggest problem with designing your own website is the time it takes to learn how to do it, and if you don't work with it regularly, you have to relearn how to do it each time you want to change something. If you do an Internet search of website designers in your local area, you might find one who is relatively inexpensive and who also will show you how to make simple changes to the text of your website so that you can regularly update it without his or her help.

Regular updating is important because search engines like Google will eventually delete websites that never change. Search engines search for recent changes and updates to websites and put them at the top of their search list. People are far more likely to click on a website on the first page of a web search than they are one that is buried on the tenth page. I have a blog as part of my website, so I put a short one or two line spiritual growth tip in there every day, and this little daily change to my website means that it will be easily found when someone does a search on say "spiritual directors of Ontario."

Having a website, whether simple or elaborate, should be an indispensable part of your advertising and employment plan. Through your website you can put your résumé, all the services you offer, upcoming events you are facilitating, and all your articles and books out there for the whole world to see. Who knows you hires you to do spiritual direction, workshops, etc.

Even if your website isn't always on the first page when someone does a search, it will be an invaluable place you can direct people to for more information. You can put your website on your letterhead, business cards and brochures for those who want to learn a lot more about you.

Your Internet service provider may be able to design and host your website and list it with an Internet search engine, or you could do a Yellow Pages or Internet search for local website designers who will take care of all this for you. For a total of six hundred dollars I got a decent twenty-two page site up and running, and my website design-er showed me how to make changes in it after he loaded "Website Editor" software onto my computer.

Again, the ability to make changes is important. Your website will quickly look out of date if you cannot eliminate old workshops from it and include upcoming ones. Also, you may want to update other parts of the website every few months as you rethink how you do your practice. Work out with your website designer whether he or she will make changes for you at a low cost, or teach you how to do it yourself.

CHAPTER SEVEN

Finding Seekers Through Social Media Networking

Since I published *Finding Seekers* in 2007, social media has obviously exploded. In 2007 Facebook and YouTube were just starting, and Skype and Twitter were unknown. Back then, most people trying to promote their practice had email, some had blogs, and even fewer had websites.

It is now not only common but expected that anyone in private practice will have a website. It will probably be best to hire a paid "techie" to develop your website, but in this chapter I will explain how to get started promoting your private practice for free using blogs, Twitter, Facebook, YouTube, and Skype.

When you first start out using social media for networking it can be very daunting, so I will keep my explanations very simple and straightforward so anyone can follow them. If you are fairly technologically advanced, you may want to skip this chapter as it may seem too elementary.

I have had my own website (www.brucetallman.com) since 2003; but now, even though I am not a techie, I have constructed my own blog and put daily inspirational thoughts on it and on the blog on my website. I also send out daily tweets on Twitter, write daily on my "wall" on Facebook, have made a short video on *Finding Seekers* for

YouTube, and do spiritual direction regularly by Skype. I have figured out how to do all these free things by myself, without hiring a techie, and I will explain how easy this is in this chapter. I am still learning myself, as everyone is, but I will give you some basic guidelines to get you started on promoting your practice through social media networking.

You may wonder "What is the point of learning all this? I will just begin to get a handle on how to use Twitter, Facebook, YouTube, and Skype, and then some new revolutionary thing will come along, and everyone will jump on that bandwagon, leaving me behind once again." It is true that there will always be new, revolutionary things developing in the digital age, but aren't you glad you got on the email, Google, and Wikipedia bandwagons? All those things have greatly expanded our possibilities, and all the social media do the same. Those things will likely never go away, and neither will blogs, Facebook, Twitter, YouTube, and Skype. They will just become, more and more, the background to daily life that we don't think twice about.

A General Recommendation About Social Media Networking

I would recommend that the best way to get into social media networking is this: first read this chapter on social media marketing/networking, preferably sitting in front of your computer and trying things out as I walk you through them step-by-step. After you have tried things out, then read a whole book on the subject and try out what it suggests. Finally, if you feel the need for it, hire someone who is a professional in this area to help you out, solve any problems you are stuck on, and refine what you already know.

I read a book first and found that I still had to learn the simplest things the hard way, that is, by going to my computer and figuring them out for myself. I am going to share with you in this chapter what I have figured out. Also, this field has developed its own language, and if you start by hiring a professional and they start talking about "hashtags" or "retweeting," you will have no idea what they are talking about. It will be like listening to a foreign language.

I have researched a number of books and the best one I found was *The Social Media Marketing Book* by Dan Zarella. The reason this book worked for me, whereas others didn't, was that Zarella includes pictures of the social media on one page, and on the facing page the text explains what that social media is about. The other books are all just text, and I know it is a cliche, but it is true that "a picture is worth a thousand words."

What I am going to write here will be a summary of some key ideas in Zarella's book, but you might want to purchase his book before you do anything. On the other hand, even with Zarella's book there will be much that you won't understand. That is why I am suggesting that you start by reading this chapter. I am going to give you a practical layman's introduction to the social media.

Whether you read the present chapter first or buy Zarella's book first, you won't really have learned anything until you get on your computer and start exploring and experimenting yourself. It is the difference between reading a book about how to swim or fix a car, and actually doing it yourself. There are a lot of things that can't be put into words, they can only be learned experientially, by actually doing them.

The key words in learning social media are the same key words for learning anything on the computer: "persistent fiddling." "Fiddling" because we basically learn anything on the computer by trying things out, making mistakes, and learning from our mistakes. "Persistent" because at some point in trying to learn this, you will become very frustrated and want to quit. However, if you can persist beyond that desire to pack it in, you will succeed. Like anything else, working with social media is easy once you know what you are doing, but the initial learning can be difficult.

Creating Your Blog

A "blog" is short for "web log." It is somewhat like a daily diary of your thoughts and activities and opinions on anything under the sun you want to write on. You can easily publish it on the Internet so that anyone in the world can read it. It is a good way to connect with lots of other people and start a dialogue with them on topics you are both interested in such as spirituality, spiritual direction, theology, scripture, etc.

Again, while you read this, it would be good to be sitting at your computer and actually do things as I direct you through them step-by–step. So, get in front of your computer and let's begin!

If you Google www.blogger.com the top two links will be www.google.com/blogger and www.blogger.com. They are the same thing and will both lead you into a website called "Blogger."

You can create your own blog in fifteen minutes or less by clicking on "Get Started." When you do that it will lead you through a simple three-step process. In Step One you create a Google account or sign in if you already have a Google account. To create an account, you type in your email and password twice, type in a display name, your gender and birthday, the verification word, accept the terms, and click "continue."

In Step Two, you name your blog, that is, you give it a title that will appear on your blog when it is published. Then you choose a blog address, that is, your blog's parking spot on the Internet, and click on "check availability," type in the verification word, and click on "Continue."

In Step Three you choose a "starter template" from eight possible ones they give you. This creates a background and format for your blog. Then click on "continue." That's all there is to it! You can start writing (posting) on your blog right away, or customize how your blog looks. If you choose to post on your blog right away, they will ask you to type in a title for the post. You might title your post "Responsibility" for example, and then in the big rectangle below the title bar you type in the content of the post. For example, the content might be "The responsibility for our life is in our own hands." You then scroll down a little farther and click on "publish post." It will then say "Your post published successfully." If you want to view how others will see your blog on the Internet, and the writing you posted on your blog, click on "View Post."

Congratulations, you have just created your own blog and put your first blog post on the Internet!

If you bookmark your blog under Google "Favorites" (top left-hand corner of Google), when you click on that bookmark it will take you to your blog. If you want to write a new post on your blog, you click on "Sign in" (top right-hand corner of your blog), type in your email and password and click on "sign in." It will take you to a page called "Dashboard." If you click on "New Post" you can write a new post and publish it to your blog.

Also on the Dashboard page you can click on "Settings" and create a description for your blog that will appear under the title, add your blog to Google listings, and choose to let Internet search engines find your blog. Then you click on "Save Settings" at the bottom of the page.

If on Dashboard you click on "Design" and then click on "Template Designer" (just below the "design" tab at the top of the page), you can change the look of your blog. (Note: it may take the "Template Designer" a minute or so to load, so be patient.)

On the left side of the Template Designer you can choose different templates, backgrounds, and layouts to suit your taste. When you click on "Apply to Blog" (upper right corner of Template Designer) your blog will have a new look.

Also from Dashboard you can create a profile of yourself that includes a description of who you are and what you do, your interests, and your contact information (phone number, email, and website if you have one). You can also add a photo of yourself.

All this will be added to your blog on the Internet. You can edit this information at any time by going to Dashboard and clicking on "Edit Profile." Once you click on "Save profile" it changes the information on your blog that is available to the public. A simple way to promote your blog is to include a link to your blog after your signature at the bottom of your emails.

Twitter

Twitter is a simple way to send brief messages to a large following of people.

When I started to think about how to access Twitter, I had the mistaken notion, as I believe a lot of people do, that Twitter was only accessible if you had a "smart phone" (phone that connects you to the Internet). I had heard many times about people sending a "tweet" (Twitter message) from their mobile phone. However, as it turns out, anyone with a computer and access to the Internet can have a Twitter account and send tweets.

A lot of people I know (even my eighteen year old daughter)

refuse to use Twitter because they see it as just another silly digital fad. There may be some truth to that, but it is undeniable that a lot of people are using Twitter since it is one more way to conveniently connect with other people, just as sending texts from your cell phone is. However, unlike text messages, tweets can be passed along instantly from computers or smart phones among large networks of friends, so they can be a way to become rapidly and widely known.

Twitter as of early 2011 boasted two hundred million users and eight hundred thousand searches daily. If you Google www.twitter.com you will get almost eleven *billion* hits (that is mentions of Twitter on the Internet).

The top hit is "twitter.com" which includes a section on "Twitter basics" which will answer every possible question you have about Twitter. I am going to give you the bare bones to get you started.

The second hit is "twitter.com/signup." Click on "Create an Account" and do what they require for you to sign up for Twitter. They will ask you to choose a Twitter address, which will be preceded by the "@" sign. Often Twitter addresses simply contain your first and last name with the last letter missing. For example, my Twitter address is "@brucetallma." If people want to find me, they simply go to the top of their Twitter home page, and in the search bar type in "Bruce Tallman" and click on the magnifying glass symbol, and on the right-hand side "brucetallma" will appear. If they click on that, my home page and all my tweets will appear.

Once you have set up an account, if you want to send a tweet, you simply go to your home page, and under "What's Happening?" type in a message. The message can only be 140 characters long, and punctuation and spaces are included as characters. It is a good idea to include your website or your blog address as the last characters of the tweet, so that people can go there is they want to. With the space before it and two dots in the middle of it, my website address www.brucetallman.com uses up 21 characters. That leaves me with 119 characters to get my message across. Twitter forces you to be concise, which is the essence of good communication, so it is a good skill to learn.

Under "What's Happening?" it's best to not type in (or text in) whatever you are doing in the moment. Unless you are famous, probably no one cares if you are sitting in a sidewalk café having a double mocha coffee. Rather, it is better to write some memorable thought or something about spiritual direction that will make people want to go to your website or your blog in order to learn more. I am slowly building followers on Twitter by doing this.

For example, this morning my tweet was "Empathy is broader than compassion. Compassion is for suffering. Empathy is to rejoice, laugh, cry, or feel compassion. www.brucetallman.com."

I put in a second tweet that said "Confused about your spiritual journey? Spiritual direction with a trained counsellor can help you sort things out. www.brucetallman.com."

When you are on your home page on Twitter, on the top bar you can click on "Profile" and then, just below where a picture would go, you can click on "Edit your profile." Under "Bio" include key words about everything you do. You only have 160 characters to describe yourself here so don't use full sentences. For example, just write "workshops" not "I facilitate workshops."

Also, under "Profile" add a real life picture of yourself, your real name, your location (just your city not your full address), and your blog or website address. Once you click on "Save," all this information will be added to your public profile and it will be given to search engines so that if people are searching for you, they can find you.

It's good to occasionally include the actual words "spiritual direction" or "spiritual director" in your tweets, so if someone does a Twitter search on these words your tweet and website address will come up. I like to write memorable thoughts daily and something about spiritual direction maybe once a week. That way I don't turn off my followers who are interested in my thoughts but not in spiritual direction, yet people can still find me if they are searching for a spiritual director. Your tweet about spiritual direction will stay on Twitter for about a week.

A few other simple things about Twitter. On the right hand side of your Twitter home page there will appear suggestions of who to "follow." You can follow other people by first of all clicking on their picture, reading the profile that comes up, and then clicking on "Follow."

Following someone means that their tweets will come up on your home page. However, they may not choose to return the favour and follow you. This explains for example why Bill Gates right now has 2,828,000 followers and he is only following 65 people himself.

Also on the right side of your home page it lists "Trends." This is a list of the most popular tweets. This can be useful for keeping in touch with current issues. It is what is on people's minds the most at any given time and can be the source of inspiration for your blog posts or articles you write. From doing a lot of writing, I have learned that what gets published is not necessarily what is most brilliant, but what is most timely in terms of peoples' current interests.

However, these "Trends" can change rapidly, so strike while the iron is hot.

You may also see tweets with the # sign in them. The # sign is called a "hashtag" and lets you follow people with similar interests. For example, I live in London, Ontario and there was a group of people concerned about the lack of bicycle paths, so the group #lonbikepath was formed and let anyone weigh in on this issue. You could create your own special interest Twitter group using hashtags like #spiritual, #clergy, #nuns, etc.

One possible way to gain followers on Twitter would be to click on the picture of those you are following and those who are your followers (mid-right side of your Twitter home page). When you click on an individual picture, that person's home page comes up. If you scroll down a bit, on the right it will show pictures of who this person is following. You could research one person after another as their brief profile comes up with their picture, trying to find people with similar interests to yours, or who you think might be interested in following you. You could then click on "Follow" under their picture on their home page and hope that some of those who you choose to follow will return the favour and follow you.

(Note: You can delete someone who you no longer want to follow by placing your cursor over "Follow" under their picture on their home page. When you do this, "Follow" will change to "Unfollow" and you simply click on this.)

Even more simply, in the top bar on your Twitter home page, to the right of where it says "Home" "Profile" and "Messages" it says

"Who to Follow." If you click on this, a list of organizations and people will come up who Twitter thinks you might want to follow based on who you already follow. However, many of these people will be famous and will probably not follow you in return. For example, the Dalai Llama has two million followers, but he himself is following no one.

If someone chooses to follow you, an email will be sent to you notifying you of this. You should follow up and thank them and choose to follow them because they may have researched you and be really interested in you and your tweets. Or they may have just randomly selected you.

In general, it appears that many people are using Twitter as a means to promote themselves, their interests, and their business. This is natural since it is free, and you should use Twitter to freely advertise your services. However, it is also important, in my judgement, to have something substantial to say in your tweets. That way you will gradually gain followers who are genuinely interested in you and what you have to say, will stick with you rather than "unfollowing" you, and will gradually be helped by you. Use Twitter not only to gain followers but, most importantly, to serve others.

Facebook

If you Google "Facebook" you will get fourteen billion hits, even more than Twitter. Facebook is the largest of all the social networking sites. As of early 2011, it had five hundred million users. Facebook has a vision of a Web tied together through personal relationships. Through your profile page you share lots of information about your interests, education, and work and thus forge online links with friends and acquaintances. The average user has about 150 "friends" through Facebook.

Facebook can be thought of as your home on the Internet where you can share photos, videos, and events of your life. Other people can go to your home page and leave messages, and browse through your photos. The "Wall" on your Facebook page is where the majority of activity takes place. People can write on your Wall and you can write on their Wall.

Facebook can also be very useful for people who are developing their private practice. Here is how to get started with Facebook.

The top hits when you Google "Facebook" are, of course, by the Facebook corporation. Under the very top hit, if you click on "Create a Page," you will be given a choice of six types of pages to choose from. You might want to choose ""Local Business or Place" or "Cause or Community." You will be asked to name your page, to agree to Facebook terms by checking off a box, and then click on "Get Started."

Under "Get Started" you can first of all add an image of yourself for your Facebook home page by clicking on "Upload an Image," which will let you browse through your computer for any stored images of yourself. After that, if you go to Step One, you can let others know about you by clicking on "Invite Your Friends," and then selecting friends by typing in their name and double clicking on their picture (if they already have a Facebook page). Facebook will recommend to them that they check out your Facebook page if you click on "Recommend."

Another way to let people know about your Facebook page is to go to Step Two "Tell your Fans" and click on "Import Contacts." The fastest way to find potential "fans" is to provide your email address and password. This is secure as it is a one-time thing, and Facebook won't store your password. Facebook will search your email address book for people who have Facebook pages, and allow you to recommend your Facebook page to them. This is easy, but it only works with the most common types of email such as Hotmail, Yahoo, Gmail, etc.

If you click on "Post Update" under Step Three, you can easily write things and post photos and videos on your Facebook home page. You can either upload photos about what you do (a photo of you sitting with a friend would simulate the spiritual direction session) that are already stored on your computer by clicking on "Upload a Photo (from your drive)" or if you have a laptop with a built-in webcam, you can easily take a photo of yourself by clicking on "Take a photo (with a webcam)."

If you want to record a video on your Facebook page, you click on "Post Update" in Step Three, and then click on "Video." When it is loaded and ready to record, your webcam will be turned on, and you simply click the square red button and start recording, and then click the square black button when you want to stop. Write something about the video below it and click on "Share" and it will save your video on your home page. It's that simple!

On the Facebook bar at the top of your Facebook home page click on "Profile" on the right side of the bar and add a photo and description of yourself: some basic information about your work, philosophy, interests, etc. You can also add your phone number, email and website under "Contact Information."

By writing on a person's Wall in Facebook you can send birthday greetings and congratulations to specific individuals and thus build a direct personal relationship with potential clients. You can also send public messages describing an event or workshop you are facilitating, and invite your friends to it.

You could build up a whole network of "friends" on Facebook by checking out the friends of your friends and requesting them to add you as a friend. A more intelligent, specific and fruitful way to go about things would be to do a search on some spiritually related word such as "meditation" or "Christian" or "prayer" and build friends with similar interests from there. If you simply try to add friends of friends, you may add a lot of people with no interest in spiritual direction.

If you do a search for people interested in spirituality and ask them to be your friend, and they respond, get to know them and make it more personal by letting them know your website and email addresses.

The age group that uses Facebook the most is people between 35 to 54 years old. Usually by then people have grown up, taken on some major responsibilities such as a family and career, been knocked around by life enough to know that life is hard, and they are more open to the idea of needing support such as spiritual direction to help them survive spiritually in the confusing spiritual wasteland of postmodern culture.

YouTube

The fourth giant player in social media networking besides blogs, Twitter, and Faceboook is YouTube. To get started in social media networking it is imperative for you to have at least some representation of what you do in all four of these avenues.

YouTube is the world's largest video-sharing community. It is a place where you can not only discover and watch videos on almost any topic under the sun, but you can also upload your own videos to YouTube and share them with the world. You can, as YouTube says "broadcast yourself."

YouTube is like putting yourself on world-wide television. When I Googled "YouTube.com" there were over 9 billion hits. A lot of people of all ages now watch more YouTube videos than they watch regular television. Instead of watching the limited number of channels you get on your television (even with cable or a satellite dish) , you can watch millons of YouTube videos. Once you get into the YouTube website, by doing a YouTube search (at the top of your computer screen), you can select and watch any video you want, on any topic you want, at any time you want!

Next to Google, YouTube is the second largest search engine in the world. It shows over two million videos to visitors to the site every day. Google bought YouTube in 2006 because of the fierce competition between the two of them.

YouTube can be a great place to explain to the world what spiritual direction is all about, and your particular approach to it. Here are some simple step-by-step instructions on how to get started doing that.

At the top right side of the "YouTube.com" home page, click on "Create account." Your YouTube account is called a "channel." Give your email address and create a "Username" and check its availability. It's important to note that you cannot change your username, so start a new business channel/account with a business name (or just use your real name). Your username determines your YouTube URL (Universal Resource Locator)—your address on YouTube, which is invaluable in directing people to your YouTube channel.

To access YouTube you have to also create a Google account, or if you already have one, just sign in to Google. Google will send you an email, and when they do you simply click on the link in the email to complete the YouTube registration process.

Once you have created your YouTube channel, your YouTube username will appear in the top right side of the YouTube screen. If you click on the two downward arrows next to your username, a box will appear that says "My Account." If under My Account you click on "Channel," your YouTube channel will appear. You can then edit things in your channel by clicking on the tabs at the top of your channel.

If you click on the "Settings" tab, you can add "Channel Tags" to your channel (see the box at the upper right). The more tags you add the better, because tags are key words that the YouTube search engine uses to find your channel. If people do a search using any of the key words you have chosen, your video will appear in their list of videos to watch. So, add tags like "spiritual direction" "prayer" "contemplation" and "peace." Add as many tags as you can think of that are related to your work. Also under "Settings" you can give a title to your channel, which is another good place to put your business name or your real name.

If you scroll down a bit when you are in your channel to where it says "Profile," just under that you can click on "edit" and then add your website or blog address, a description of what your channel is about, and under "About Me" you can add a description of yourself, your interests, the type of work you do, and additional contact information such as your email address and phone number.

General Tips About Making a YouTube Video

First of all, shorter is always better. If a viewer has a choice between watching two videos on the same topic, and one is 90 seconds long and the other is ten minutes long, he or she will invariably first choose the shorter one. In any case, for standard free accounts, the top limit for uploaded videos is fifteen minutes. Less is more, because brevity forces you to really think about what you want to say, organize it carefully, and cut out any unnecessary words.

Make your videos as engaging as possible by putting energy into your talk, speaking clearly and smiling a lot. No one wants to watch a grumpy–looking, mumbling, talking head who blathers on and on.

Be aware of the background behind you. It should be simple, not overly busy. Books in the background will make you look educated, religious pictures (depending on what they are) may make you look overly-churchy or fundamentalist, one or two pictures of nature scenes can be nice, but perhaps a blank wall behind you is the least distracting background. If you have a laptop it probably has a web camera (and web camera software) built into it.

Remember that the screen to the viewer will look two dimensional not three dimensional—it can look like a thing (such as a lamp) behind you is actually coming out of your head! Also, be aware of the angle the camera is shooting from, and how close you are to it. Do you really want people to see that double chin of yours (which will show up if you have your laptop in your lap)?

Since you don't have a TelePrompTer, it's a good idea to have a short memorized speech. So write out your speech and time it and then break it down into key points, group those points under three or so major headings, memorize the major headings and subheadings, and then practice "spontaneously" delivering your speech three or four times before you record it for YouTube.

Keep your videos non-commercial, not a pitch to buy your book, attend your workshop, or take spiritual direction with you. You might want to talk about different ways of praying, or the difference between contemplation and meditation, or how to use the Enneagram for spiritual growth.

How To Upload A YouTube Video

Here is a simple step–by-step process to follow while in front of your computer.

First of all, click on your YouTube bookmark. When YouTube comes up, click on "Upload" (just to the right of the "Search" bar). You can then either upload a video that is already on your computer by clicking on "Upload Video," or you can record a video right now by clicking on "Record from webcam" which will activate the webcam built into your laptop or the webcam plugged into your computer.

When you click on "Record from webcam," a box will come up with some choices in it. Click on "Allow" and when (or if) another box comes up, click on "Allow" again, which will access any web-cam/video recording software on your computer. It may not detect your software immediately, so you may have to click on "Retry" if it says no camera was found.

Once the "Ready to Record" button comes up, center yourself on the screen, remember your prepared talk, and then click on the grey "Ready to Record" button and begin recording. Hit the "Stop" button (red square at lower left) when you are finished recording. Then click on "Publish."

Fill in the "Title" box, the "description" box, add as many "Tags" as possible, and pick the "Category" you want your video to be in. They don't have a category for "spiritual direction" or even "religion" or "spirituality," but you might choose the "education" or "how to" or "people and blogs" category. Then scroll to the bottom and check on "save changes."

A page will come up that says "Video details have been updated!" If you scroll down on this page until you get to "Video Thumbnail," you can choose one of three video still photography shots that will be the still image people will see if they search for videos in the category you chose on YouTube. Once you have chosen the still image you want, click on "Save Changes." Then click on the "Play" button to see how your video will look on YouTube.

If you are not satisfied you can re-record your video or make a different video. To edit your video's title, description, and tags, go to your account and click on "videos" and then click on "edit" beside the video.

Once you have a satisfactory video recorded and saved on YouTube, close YouTube, and then go back into YouTube and do a search for your video using the title you chose in order to see if others could find it on YouTube. Your video should come up at the top of the list.

Congratulations—you now have your first video up and running on YouTube!

After you upload your video to YouTube, you could post it, or at least write about it, on your website, blog, or Facebook page, and email your friends, family, and clients about it.

Skype

No discussion of social media would be complete without mentioning Skype. However, as with the rest of the social media, if you have never used it before, it may seem daunting to know how to begin with Skype. Here is a simplified introduction.

Hundreds of millions of people are using Skype, and so Skype is starting to revolutionize the way spiritual direction is done. With Skype you can not only talk to people anywhere in the world for free, you can see them on your computer screen, as long as you both have downloaded Skype onto your computers. I now do spiritual direction by Skype with people in California, Quebec, Cape Cod, Philadelphia, and New York, and my own spiritual director lives in Denver, Colorado.

If it works properly, Skype can be better than doing spiritual direction by phone, and almost as good as being there with them in person. You can see the directee's nonverbal reactions, which you obviously cannot do by phone.

However, Skype can be unpredictable, and it sometimes happens that it shuts off in the middle of a session, or the person's voice fades out, or their face freezes or even breaks up so it looks something like a Picasso painting! In these cases, it is better to do distance spiritual direction by phone. When Skype is not working properly it can be extremely frustrating.

To help it work properly, it is important to shut down any other programs you have running, disconnect everything that is plugged into the USB ports on your computer, and make sure that the power settings on your computer aren't dimming the screen or sending the computer into sleep mode. The quality of Skype can also be affected by the quality of your webcam and that of the person at the other end. The quality of webcams built into laptops may be questionable in some cases, and so it may be important to buy a high quality USB webcam that you can plug into your laptop. Also, if you are on a wifi network the transmission can be of lesser quality than if you are directly plugged into the Internet by phone line or cable.

Part of the problem with transmission may be that the number of people streaming movies and videos is constantly increasing and so the entire Internet may be reaching the point of overload. Millions more will probably start using Skype, and so the system may continue to be overwhelmed and cause connection problems, but assuming that the Skype technology gets better and better, Skype is another very useful tool to have in your repertoire of social media capabilities. So here is a step-by-step guide to get started with Skype.

To start using Skype, go to www.skype.com and follow the simple instructions to download the latest free Skype software. Once you have done that, go to "Tools" on the top bar of your Skype page, click on "Options" and then on "Video Settings," which will activate the web camera built-in or plugged into your computer. You can then adjust the webcam settings to get a clear webcam video of yourself that the person on the other end will see.

By clicking on the Echo/Sound Test Service in your "Contacts" list, you can see if your computer microphone is working properly, and hear yourself as the person at the other end will hear you.

Then, click on "Contacts" in the top bar, and click on "Add a Contact." If you know the email of the person you want to Skype with, you just need to enter it into the box provided, and Skype will track down their Skype page and add their name to your contact list. Skype will then prompt you to send the person a message asking them to accept you as a Skype contact. If they accept, you will be added to their Skype contact list, and then you are ready to begin Skyping with them.

If you click "Skype" and then on "Online Status" it will tell you what the various symbols in front of the names of the people in your contact list mean.

By email you then work out with the other person when you both want to be on Skype together. Since you can Skype with anyone in the world, you need to take their time zone and yours into account. When you get together at your agreed upon time, you double click on their name on your contact list, and then click on "Video Call" and Skype will connect you when they click on "Answer Call."

As well as seeing them, you will see a small picture of yourself, so you know how they are seeing you at the other end. You may have to adjust the angle of your screen or move your chair so that your face is in the center of the screen. As with YouTube, be aware of the background behind you. Again, a plain background is probably the best.

As far as payment for distance spiritual direction goes, if you both have a PayPal account, the directee can pay you using PayPal. PayPal accepts major credit cards if they prefer to pay you that way. The other option would be for them to snailmail you a certified cheque or money order. However, PayPal is far more convenient and quick.

If you become proficient at using Skype, it will vastly expand your possiblities for doing spiritual direction. You no longer have to be in a city with a large enough population base to support your spiritual direction practice. You can be living by yourself in the countryside, off in the middle of nowhere, and still sustain your practice because, as long as you have access to the Internet, you can connect with people in the major urban centers, and indeed with anyone anywhere.

What I Do For Social Networking

On maybe four days of the week, I first go to Twitter and enter a short, 140 character tweet. I copy this tweet to the blog on my website, and then copy it as a post on my blog "Spiritual Direction with Bruce Tallman." Then I copy it on my wall on Facebook. So, in a matter of ten minutes, I have made changes to all these sites.

This makes it easy for search engines to find my sites and put them at the top of the list when someone does an Internet search. Since I started doing this little exercise a lot more people have said they found me online. So, it is worth my time because of the new people becoming my directees.

It took me several months to figure all this out, but you can go ahead and use this method for recruiting seekers right away, once you get your blog, Twitter, and Facebook sites set up.

CHAPTER EIGHT

Keeping Seekers (Ethically)

Here in the city of London, Ontario there is a paramedic who has become a very wealthy man. When the *London Free Press* interviewed him and asked him the secret of his wealth, he said, "It's not how much money you bring in that counts, it's how much you keep."

As spiritual counselors we are interested in the spiritual transformation of people, not becoming wealthy, but the same principle holds: "It is not how many clients you *get,* but how many you *keep,* that builds a spiritual direction practice."

Now, it is important to be careful here. You do not want to keep clients when it is clearly the will of the Higher Power that they move on. You don't want to interfere with what the Higher Power is doing in a person's life.

However, there are times when you know that it would do a client a lot of good to keep coming, but you also know that they are probably going to stop seeing you. This can be for a variety of reasons: first of all, you may be getting very close to painful truths in their life that they don't want to face. Psychologists are familiar with this phenomenon: just when they are getting closest to a breakthrough in therapy their client quits because the client knows that if they keep coming they are going to have to make some big changes in their life.

Secondly, some clients are unmotivated and lazy about their spiritual life and will stop coming at the slightest whim. Others are overly busy or easily distracted and their spiritual life easily gets put on the back burner. Still others expect every session to be an amazing experience, and when that doesn't always happen, they quit.

If you wish to keep clients, it is imperative that you keep them through ethical practices so that they freely choose to keep coming to see you out of a sense of all the benefits they are receiving, and not because of any manipulation on your part.

Prayer

The first thing to do in keeping clients is to pay attention to your own prayer and meditation life. If you are connecting deeply with your Higher Power in your own prayer life you will be a much better spiritual counselor, the Higher Power's love will freely flow from you to the client, and the client's deepest need, to be loved, will be met. Again, our first responsibility to our clients is to love them. If you are holding yourself and your clients before your Higher Power there will be a spiritual bond formed between you. The best way to ensure that your clients' spiritual needs are being met is to regularly engage in intercessory prayer for them. In addition to prayer, there are many practical things you can do.

Initial Phone Contact

It is possible to lose clients right at their first phone call to you. It is best at this point to first do a lot of listening rather than talking. This allows you to get to know where they are coming from and how to frame your questions and answers to them. Inquire as to why they are interested in spiritual counseling, what their needs and concerns are, and then tell them if you genuinely think you can help them. Remember that people are more interested in how spiritual counseling is going to benefit them than they are in all your degrees or services, so frame your conversation that way, without making unrealistic (and therefore unethical) claims. The key thing is to build an atmosphere of trust with your inquirer.

It is also important to set up a session as soon as you can—the same day or the next day if possible, even if this is really inconvenient for you and you have to work extra hours and quit work later than usual. If you set the session up a week or two away they will often change their minds about coming to spiritual counseling. It is important to set things up while they are in the right mood because moods can change rapidly.

Also, in spite of your best efforts to reassure them in the initial phone call, many people will be quite nervous about baring their soul to another human being, particularly if they have never done it before and they don't really know you. I usually send them a reassuring email right after the initial phone contact.

If you are absolutely booked up and have to set up the first session a week away, phone them the night before to confirm the meeting. Be sure to get their phone number and permission to phone them when they first phone you. Some people do not want their other family members (particularly their spouses or partners) to know they are seeing a spiritual counselor.

Their other family members may question them on it, think it is unnecessary, feel threatened by it, or, since most people don't know what spiritual direction is, think it is something weird. If they don't want you to phone them, ask for their email, and, if they give you permission to contact them in this way, send them an email the day before. Keep in mind that they may not want you to do this either because some family members share the same email address.

When I first started, I used to phone everyone the night before to remind them of the meeting next day. By now, most of my directees have been with me for a long time (some for over ten years) and most of them are regular attenders who I know will be there. However, there are certain personality types (usually the "p's" on the Myers Briggs—the spontaneous people) who, even though they have been coming for a long time, still need reminding of the upcoming session.

When you first start out, an alternative to phoning the night before would be to have a list of all your directee's emails and on the weekend send the following email to everyone you have an appointment with in the week ahead: "Dear (their name), I am looking forward to our meeting on (date and time)."

Set Up Tentative Appointments

This is very important: try to set up *tentative* appointments with people. People who phone you to inquire about spiritual direction will often say, after you have talked for a while, "Okay, I'll think about doing a session. I'll get back to you." If they say "I'll get back to you," they usually won't, so say "Why don't we set up a tentative appointment? If you change your mind you can just call me back and cancel the appointment." This works because it is easier for them to not get back to you than to call you and cancel a tentative appointment you have already set up.

In my experience people often seem relieved that they have actually set up a tentative appointment. They realize they are actually going to move ahead with their spiritual growth, not just think about it.

The First Session

Hospitality is what spiritual direction is all about, so be hospitable in every session, but be particularly aware of being hospitable in the first and second sessions. Most people decide whether to keep coming after the second session. If the first session did not go well, they will usually give you the benefit of the doubt—maybe you were out of sorts and the first session was an aberration—so they will come to the second session with the hope of dispelling their initial judgement. However, if the second session also does not go well, their negative judgement will have been confirmed and they won't be back.

In the first session, invite them to talk about their story before you describe how you approach spiritual direction. This allows you to get to know them better and to adjust what you say about your services to who they are and what they need.

I usually don't start the first session with a prayer because I do not know yet if they pray or value prayer. However, I ask permission to close the first session with a prayer if, from what they have told me about themselves, I think they would feel comfortable with it. I generally try to sum up three key points from the session in my closing prayer so they can take these points with them. That way they can easily think about what they got out of the session.

In future sessions, if they are comfortable with prayer, I start with a prayer, end with a prayer, and pray during the sessions, if I think it is appropriate. If the client does not feel comfortable with being prayed for (most people welcome it), I just pray silently anyway.

After the closing prayer I take their contact information and give them a copy of my office policies to read at home. Among other things, the office policies tell them how they can benefit the most from the sessions, for example, taking notes in the session or after it. It also gives them questions to ask themselves about their spiritual life before the next session, so that they come to the sessions prepared with issues they want to discuss.

A strong start with clients is important so that they experience the benefits of spiritual direction as early as possible in the process. Giving them your total attention is important in any session, but I believe it is particularly important in the first few sessions when they are forming a new habit, that is, regularly attending spiritual direction sessions.

This is just my approach, and some spiritual directors do not do this, but, if I sense that a client is open to it, I give them a fair amount of homework to begin with—a questionnaire that helps them develop a spiritual autobiography, or I give them particular scriptural readings, or the Myers Briggs Type Indicator to fill out and mail back to me, and so on. Once they are in the habit of regularly coming to spiritual direction, I may give them less homework or not, depending upon what I judge to be appropriate. On the other hand, I may not give them anything for the first few sessions and start giving them homework later. Some directees love homework, others hate it. Usually it depends upon how busy their life already is.

Advantages And Disadvantages Of Taking Notes

I believe that taking notes after each session is one of the keys to keeping clients. You may think this is unnecessary as you will remember the broad themes of the person's spiritual journey when you meet, and this may be so. However, I constantly find that I am reminded of a lot of important things about the previous session that I would have forgotten if I had not taken notes.

I limit myself to seven minutes of note-taking after the client leaves, and then I jot three main points from these notes in the margin. I can then easily review the main points of this session before the next session. I can also easily review the main points from sessions held in the past six months or longer and see patterns I would have missed if I had not taken notes. I also find that I get many new insights about the client while writing and reviewing my notes, and many more insights between sessions than I would have without notes.

Although some directors may think that taking notes is a waste of time, I believe it is more efficient and time-saving than not taking notes. This is because clients feel like I have really listened to them if I am able to bring up key issues from the last session or from a few sessions ago. This helps me to keep clients and so I spend less time looking for clients and spend more time actually working with them. It takes much more effort to find a client than to keep one.

Some directors may object that reviewing notes from the last session just before the present one will get in the way of being totally open to where the client is now. Over the course of a month the client may go through big changes, and you won't be ready for this if you have your head stuck back in the previous session. I agree with this assessment. So, I keep the three points from the previous session on the backburner of my mind, and go into the present session with my heart and mind wide open in order to receive wherever the client is now.

I give my total attention to, and go with the flow of, where the client is at in this particular moment of time. However, if the session seems to be really bogged down and going nowhere, I ask about key points from previous sessions, if the opportunity presents itself. For example, I might say "I remember that a close friend of yours died six months ago. What impact has that had on your faith or your spiritual life since then?"

Sometimes, if it seemed like a particularly hard session, I will spend an additional three minutes taking notes about myself and my reactions to the session. This also helps when I prepare for the next session. I am aware of my possible reactions before they happen and therefore make sure they don't interfere with my openness to the client. I can also use these notes as a basis for conversations with my supervisor or peer supervision group.

All notes should be kept strictly confidential, under lock and key when not being used, and with no marks on them which would identify to whom they are referring.

Closing Comments Are Crucial

In keeping directees/clients/seekers what you say at the end of a session can determine your success or failure. I never say "Do you want to meet again?" or "When do you want to meet again?"

If you ask "Do you want to meet again?" you are inviting them to give a "yes" or "no" response. You are basically inviting them to quit, when the option of quitting may have been the furthest thing from their mind. They may never have considered quitting, but now you are forcing them to think about it.

If you ask "when do you want to meet again?" you are inviting them to make their sessions much more spread out. With most seekers you will establish a pattern early on of how often you meet. If you have been meeting once every two weeks, they may say "let's meet a month from now." If you have been meeting once a month, they may say, "let's meet in 3 months."

If we have established a pattern of meeting every week, I get out my planning book and say "next week I could meet you on Tuesday at 1:30pm." If we have established a pattern of meeting once a month, I say "let's see, four weeks from today would take us to (date). I could see you that day at (time)." If we have established a pattern of meeting every two or three months I might say "Spiritual direction tends to lose its impact if you meet less than once a month. Are you sure you want to keep meeting that infrequently?"

Again, you have to be very cognizant of what the directee/seeker can or cannot afford. You don't want spiritual direction to become a financial burden for them. I have some directees who I see every three months and they pay me $20 because that is what they can afford, and I treat them just as well as the rich person who wants to see me every week and pay $85. On the other hand, I really believe in the value of spiritual direction, and so if I think a person can afford it, I will ask if they want to meet more often.

For most seekers though, if we have established a pattern, I just assume they want to stick with that pattern, rather than asking them questions that might cause them to quit or thin out how often we meet.

Reviews

Every six months, or whenever I feel it is warranted, I will review with clients how the sessions have been going for them. I do this by tactfully reading my notes back to them month by month, and asking them to comment after each month. This helps them (and me) see the progress they have made. I am careful to not read back anything I think would be inappropriate for them to hear. We then go through a "Spiritual Direction Evaluation" form together.

It is important to say to your client before you begin the review that it is good to periodically go over where they have been and discuss what they might want to work on with you from here on. Say up front that the purpose of the review is not to end the sessions or criticize them. Otherwise, there is a danger when you say you want to do a review that the client will think this is your final session and you are doing the review because you want to wrap things up, or you don't like working with them and want to criticize them.

So be sure to make it clear *why* you are doing the review, that it is so that you can continue to work *even more effectively* together. The review also provides the client with the opportunity to voice any concerns or complaints (or praise!) they have been secretly harboring, lets you know how they are experiencing the sessions, and gives you an opportunity to praise their progress. I know it is hard to measure spiritual "progress," but I mean things like the client is praying more regularly, more at peace with himself or herself and others, etc. This will always be a subjective judgement on your part, but when you go through your notes the progress is usually fairly obvious.

Focus On Benefits And Results

Focus your promotional materials (brochures, newsletters, websites, advertising, business cards) mainly on the benefits and results of spiritual direction. Do not just list the features of your practice, the services you provide, and your degrees and publications. People are most interested in the benefits they will personally receive. This cannot be stressed enough.

If you talk to clients regularly about results you and they see, it helps them justify to themselves and others the cost of the sessions. Clearly articulating their progress in occasional reviews will make it more likely that they will continue coming.

In fact, you could ask them at the end of each session "What were the key things you got out of today's session?" You could also, when you make notes after each session, list any results, new behaviors, or new attitudes you have noticed, and share these with the client in the next session. What people often need, more than anything else, is simply encouragement and the feeling that they have been heard and are making progress.

It is important to talk to clients every six months, three months, or even once a month about the results you see even if you don't do a full-fledged review. If you wait too long, and only give them feedback on their progress when you evaluate things in the final termination or closure session, you will miss a lot of subtle changes that happened along the way.

Reflecting regularly on the results that spiritual direction is producing will not only keep your clients motivated, it will also motivate you and make you feel like all your efforts have been worthwhile. At the same time, there are often subterranean and subtle things happening in the depths of the client's soul that neither you nor the client are aware of and that may not visibly surface till months later, so don't feel discouraged if there are not many immediately tangible results.

Focusing on results will also give you some stories about how your work really helped someone, so that, when people ask what you do, you can tell them in a conversational (rather than academic) tone of voice, by giving them some concrete examples of how you have helped people.

Remember to omit any details that might enable other people to identify who your clients are. I usually tell people up front that I am changing names and identifying details to protect confidentiality.

Also remember to speak clearly without any technical jargon, and don't over-promise benefits and results or you will lose credibility. Just state honest results and remember that if you put ethics first, everything else will be taken care of by your Higher Power.

Your Enthusiasm

If you obviously take pleasure in your work and are enthusiastic about it, it will rub off on your clients and they will be more likely to stay with you. If you are obviously burned out, clients will flee. So, you have to take care of yourself and lead a balanced life. It is important therefore to have your own spiritual director, supervisor or peer supervision group, and perhaps a good therapist.

You could also ask yourself if your schedule of appointments includes things that re-invigorate you, such as study, professional development workshops, retreats, and holidays, or is your schedule exhausting or boring you? I will say more about this later.

You could develop a profile of your "Ideal Client" and search for this type of person if you feel constantly frustrated with your present clients. For me, the ideal client would be someone who has already done a lot of inner work, and who is serious about the spiritual life. Often, when I least expect it, my Higher Power will send me clients who are a good match for me.

Also ask yourself if you are happy with the surroundings you work in: are they cheerful and ergonomic, practical, and comfortable? Do they work for you by providing a healthy environment that lifts your spirits? Or are they dilapidated, poorly lit, too business-like, etc?

Hiring an interior designer who knew something about "feng shui," that is, how our surroundings block or facilitate our energy flow, helped me a lot. For a modest fee, she recommended getting more comfortable couches, bookshelves and a wicker room divider that blocked my desk, filing cabinets, and computer off from the counseling area, as well as getting rid of an old television that served no useful purpose. We purchased a Japanese bowl and filled it with white sand and sea shells as a centerpiece, put up some spirituality posters, and got a colorful Navajo rug to put on top of the plain gray carpet. Now my counseling room feels like it is set up for intimate sharing and I am proud to invite individuals, couples, and groups into it.

To maintain your excitement about your work, ask yourself if you are constantly learning and being creative in the spiritual methods you teach and the workshops you do? Does your work embody your real passions and values or are you bored and just going through the motions? The nonverbal communication you are giving your clients can have a big impact on whether they stay or go.

Extra-Ordinary Contact and Home Visits

If you believe or intuit that someone is about to quit coming to spiritual counseling, when it would really be to their benefit to continue, some form of contact outside of the sessions may help. Again, you need to be careful that you are not interfering with the Higher Power's work in this person. If you are quite certain it would be appropriate, you might send the person a note of encouragement, or a card, or email articles, poems, or information about helpful and relevant websites.

You might also want to consider doing home visits if the client wants spiritual direction but doesn't want to do it by phone, cannot travel, and lives within a reasonable driving distance. The client then just pays for your travel costs in addition to your fee. I have one long-term client who does not have a car and could not easily get to my office, whereas I can get to her house in five minutes by car, so I drive to her home. Another client was gradually going blind, could no longer drive her car, and was spending a small fortune on taxis, so I offered to come to her house. Do not go anywhere unless you know that the client feels comfortable with it. When entering another person's home as a spiritual counselor you have to be very aware of liability and boundary violation issues, on both your part and that of the client.

Jesus encouraged his followers to go the extra mile with people, and I have found that spiritual counseling often affords an excellent opportunity to literally do that.

Distance Spiritual Direction

If people are too distant to drive or are snowed in during the winter, you could offer to do spiritual direction with them by email or by phone. I have found that people are glad to have this opportunity, and I have done spiritual counseling by email with several people. Sometimes people feel more comfortable expressing themselves in writing. They are more able to access and express their real thoughts and feelings through writing than talking. Certainly, people who are introverts on the Myers-Briggs would be more inclined this way than extroverts. One downside of doing spiritual direction by email is that, if you are a slow typist, it can take a lot longer to type something than to say it.

Spiritual direction by phone can also work. I have engaged in spiritual direction by phone with people as far away as the Yukon and West Virginia. One advantage it has over spiritual direction by email is that you can tell a lot about what a person is feeling by the tone of their voice. It also has the advantage over in-person spiritual direction of being pure listening without any visual distractions. However, there is the disadvantage of not being able to read the client's nonverbal behavior.

If you or your clients have a low cost phone plan or use phone cards, long distance bills can cost as little as two or three dollars an hour. I have a phone plan I pay a certain basic amount for, but once I have paid that, I can phone all over North America for free. If there are any long distance costs for you as the spiritual counselor, you will need to work out with the client who would pay for these. It should probably be the client, but use your own judgement as to what is appropriate.

As mentioned earlier, another possibility is for you and your client to both download free Skype or Windows Live Messenger software to your computers and buy headsets and a web camera, so that you can talk long distance and see each other on your computer screen. Other than the headset and camera, there is no cost in doing this, no connection or long distance charges, and it is the next best thing to being in the room with each other.

However, it can also have some drawbacks. If your client buys a cheap ($20-$30) webcam, the transmission of their facial features can be poor. I usually encourage clients to spend twenty or thirty dollars more in order to purchase a USB webcam which will eliminate this problem.

Another problem is that the camera might cut out during the session. Skype seems to be more reliable than Messenger in this regard. There can also be problems with the client's lack of computer skills, or with sound and lighting. USB cameras often have built in microphones, and if you bought computer speakers, you would not have to use a headset.

As the technology improves, distance spiritual direction through the Internet is becoming more and more commonplace. With laptop computers, you can both be sitting in the comfort of your living rooms thousands of miles apart and having a face-to-face live spiritual direction chat.

Generating Loyalty

Having clients who are loyal to you comes from clients feeling that their needs are being met. This requires genuine *listening* on your part. It is important to give clients *what they want and need, not what you think they need*. For example, you may think they need to know their Enneagram type, but they may have no interest in this. If, because of your enthusiasm for the Enneagram, you try to force this upon them, when what they really want is to learn some new ways of praying so that they can revive their spiritual life after a long drought, they may decide to vote with their feet and not come back.

It is important to distinguish their needs from their wants. They might want to spend their time in spiritual counseling sharing their narrow religious views while you are discerning that what they need, and what the Higher Power wants you to do, is to challenge them on this, helping them to grow by broadening their spiritual outlook. Again though, you have to be careful that you are not imposing your agenda on them.

Keeping clients involves going beyond being merely ethical to developing strong ties with them so that they are more than satisfied with your work and actively promote it to others. If clients are loyal enough to refer other people to you, you know you are building a strong practice. Word of mouth comes from clients feeling not just *appreciative* of your services but *excited* about them.

Loyalty happens when counselors and clients enjoy working with each other and there is a sense that Spirit is flowing in the sessions, watering and enriching the client's spiritual life so that it is becoming more and more fertile. If the sessions are done in an environment of hospitality that welcomes the client, and the sessions combine discipline, seriousness, and rigor with the energy of laughter, pleasure, and fun, clients will enthusiastically endorse you to anyone who will listen.

Added Value

There are many ways that you can add value, that is, provide additional opportunities for growth beyond just the spiritual counseling sessions, so that the client will get the most out of his or her association with you, keep coming back, and keep recommending you to others.

Counselors could introduce clients to the Myers Briggs Type Indicator and the Enneagram in order to help them discern their spiritual strengths and areas where growth is needed. Spiritual directors could also do what I do and email all their past and present clients a "Top Ten Spiritual Growth Ideas" list each month. They could stock their waiting room with books, CDs and DVDs that clients could borrow without paying a fee. That way the client's transformation can continue between sessions.

There are many excellent spiritual growth programs that could help form clients, such as *The Nineteenth Annotation* based on the Spiritual Exercises of St. Ignatius; *The Cup of Our Life* by Joyce Rupp; *The Purpose Driven Life* by Rick Warren; *Experiencing the Heart of Jesus* by Max Lucado, etc. If clients get into these ongoing programs, it can ensure that they keep coming and you have a stable client base. However, again, do not try to manipulate your clients into taking things that they really are not interested in. You have to constantly put their needs before your needs and let the Higher Power guide you as to what you give them.

To stay vital it helps if each year your practice expands in terms of the services you offer to clients. You could start ongoing spirituality groups, write articles or self-published books on spirituality, or make your own spirituality CDs or DVDs that clients can buy from you at low cost.

You could offer a wide range of workshops on spirituality which create a fun, energetic, and laughter-filled environment for clients. You could plan to add a new service every six months or year. However, be careful not to add too much too fast or you will be overwhelmed.

A good way to add value is to attend spiritual growth workshops that nourish you, and then bring back from these workshops new ideas you can use to expand your practice. You could even offer a similar workshop, as long as you rearrange things and add enough of your own material and ideas so you avoid plagiarism.

Facilitating a spirituality group can be less time-consuming than facilitating a workshop, since groups focus less on content and therefore require less preparation time. On the other hand, facilitating a workshop can be easy if you design your workshops so that they can be easily repeated, perhaps with a new title, and a few minor changes.

You could think big and invite your clients and others to come and hear well-known spiritual teachers whom you invite to give workshops. Or you could start a monthly or bimonthly guest lecturer series. There are probably several noted wise men or wise women who live right in your area. Your clients could share in their sessions with you how all these things are impacting them.

Another way of adding value is to become a kind of clearing house for spiritual resources, that is, help your clients connect with other sources of information, other resources, and other agencies, institutions, or practitioners who could help them. You could recommend spiritually-oriented bookstores, spirituality groups, churches or other places of worship, and upcoming workshops on spirituality by others that your clients may not have heard of.

You could consult with each of your clients on programs they would like you to run. When people get together at your workshops, encourage them to form new friendships with the others there. Often this can be done simply by offering coffee before, during, or after the session so people have a chance to socialize.

You could educate yourself about a client's issue that keeps coming up: alcoholism, emotional disorders, and so on. You could learn about these problems through searching the Internet, taking courses, or doing your own reading. You will probably, in the course of your research, come across resources on this issue that you could pass on to your client to study on their own. You may also get a better sense of when you are in over your head and need to refer your client to an expert in that area.

In spite of your best efforts to keep clients, there will still be ongoing attrition, so you will need to do ongoing recruitment. At some point however, those who stay will outnumber those who leave and, as you become more adept at both finding and keeping seekers, you will have a solid and ever-growing base of committed, ongoing people. Once you get to this point, you begin to get a growing sense of security and assurance that, if someone quits, it is not going to destroy your whole practice, not everyone is going to quit at once, and you are going to continue on no matter what. Once you sense this, you begin to relax and enjoy your practice a lot more, and this relaxation releases new creative energies in you that further ensure the ongoing success of your practice.

CHAPTER NINE

Growing Your Practice

Is Your Practice Professional Or Not?

Spiritual directors and counselors, whether part-time or full-time, can operate their practice professionally or non-professionally. It should be noted that I am not referring here to the effectiveness or ineffectiveness, or to the quality or lack of quality, of your spiritual direction or counseling skills per se. What I am referring to here is how you run your practice.

You could be a very effective spiritual director/counselor and not have all of the professional practice requirements below, and still have lots of clients. However, the best situation would be to *both* be an effective counselor *and* to run your practice in a professional manner. Here are some of the differences in a professionally run versus non-professionally run practice:

Professional Practice	Non-Professional Practice
• has a plan to guide decisions about the practice	• no plan, just takes things as they come
• has goals and steps to achieve them	• no goals

Professional Practice	Non-Professional Practice
• has a business coach or mentor	• operates on his or her own
• is organized	• not particularly organized
• strengthens the practice every day	• not interested in growing stronger
• gives office policies to clients	• no office policies
• has an office and waiting room	• has a couple of chairs or a couch
• has boundaries re: work hours, incoming phone calls, missed sessions, etc.	• has no boundaries
• educates clients about his or her expectations of them and how they can benefit the most	• does not expect anything from clients
• manages time well: spends 70% of time in sessions, doing workshops, writing, and 30% networking, marketing, administration	• works on spiritual direction 1 or 2 hours per day at most
• works only with dedicated clients	• works with anyone, dedicated or not
• has an advisory board	• no advisory board

Those who work at their spiritual direction or counseling practice professionally are more likely to grow their practice and survive in the long run.

Going Public

A spiritual counseling practice, like a private social work or psychology practice, can be isolating because it is done one-to-one and is private and confidential work. Failure in running a spiritual counseling practice can often come, not from lack of effort, but from letting yourself get too isolated. In other words, it is not just what you know or who you know that helps you succeed in your practice, it's how many people know you or at least have heard about you.

There are a number of ways to overcome isolation, but you might start by thinking about your own manner of presenting yourself. How you come across may make you attract people or repel them. Are you casual or formal in your appearance? Do you smile and make eye contact too little? Are you relaxed or stiff? Approachable or intimidating? Shy or outgoing? Do you feel comfortable with yourself and others? Do they feel comfortable with you?

You could overcome isolation by connecting with other professionals: ministers, priests, psychotherapists, social workers, and so on. If you took one person a week to coffee or lunch, after a year you would have fifty new sources who might refer people to you.

You could expand your contacts by taking classes in new interests and hobbies (birdwatching, cooking, gardening, whatever you find stimulating) and joining groups that would bring you into new circles of people.

In some ways, networking to increase the quantity of people who know of you involves two interrelated skills: the ability to make small talk, and the ability to make acquaintances, not just close friends. Small talk and making casual acquaintances come easily if you keep up with current events by reading weekly news magazines.

To become well-known in the field of spiritual counseling you need to write, speak, and teach. There are online writing courses that could help you publish articles and books, and Toastmasters International (www.toastmasters.org) can help you develop speaking and teaching skills. You might also try to become part of a speakers bureau or some other organization that helps find appropriate speakers for events.

Expand Through Finding Your Niche

If you feel that you have gradually become stuck in working with only a certain type of client, and you want to start working with others, you could do this by specializing your services. For example, you could work with all types of clients by becoming known as a spiritual director who specializes in helping people in one of these areas: discernment, dream work, the Enneagram, prayer methods, developing a spiritual discipline, etc.

You may need to spend ten percent of your annual income at first getting additional training and attending workshops and conferences in the area of your choice so that you become a total expert in this area, but once you have done this, this becomes your "niche."

The above areas of specialty could be applied to people from any walk of life or background. For example, if you become an expert on discernment, you could help business people, high school or university students, scientists, teachers, religious people, atheists, or people who are "spiritual but not religious" how to make wise, life-giving choices. If you became an adept at the Enneagram, you could help all these people understand their true motivations and hidden world views, and so help them become more integrated and conscious.

Expand Through Diversification

Just as you can expand your practice through finding your niche, you can also expand it by doing the opposite, that is diversification. Diversifying what you do can have many benefits. First of all, if you were just doing spiritual direction and nothing else, it may become boring for you. So you might want to supplement it with a wide range of workshops, talks, and retreats on spiritual topics of all kinds; with meditation groups; newsletters, articles, and books; supervision of people training to be spiritual directors; scripture or adult religious education classes; life coaching or spiritual psychotherapy; consultation with businesses on how to develop spirituality at work; etc. Again, you may need to spend some time and money getting yourself trained and up to speed in these areas if you do not already have expertise.

Diversification can also be very beneficial for your clients as it allows them the freedom to choose from a menu of your services so they can develop an individualized program for themselves. Within the spiritual direction part of your practice they could choose from different prayer styles; focus on different programs like Max Lucado's *Experiencing the Heart of Jesus*, or the *Spiritual Exercises of St. Ignatius*, or Rick Warren's *The Purpose Driven Life*; then work with the Myers-Briggs Personality Inventory, or with the Enneagram. They could borrow your articles, books, and audio-visual resources, and attend workshops you give or meditation groups you facilitate.

You could have a list of all the services that you provide and ask the client to book an hour and a half for the first session. When they arrive you could give them a menu of services to read over along with your office policies. After this first half hour in your waiting room, both of you could spend an hour choosing a personalized mix of services for the client that would maximize their spiritual growth. For example, one client might choose to do spiritual direction, marriage coaching, select certain books or articles to read, and another client might choose to be in a men's spirituality group, do spiritual psychotherapy on his anxiety problems, and learn centering prayer.

Diversification can also help your cash flow during slow times. For example, if some of your clients are going to be away for holidays in the summer, or if they want to skip spiritual direction in December, July, and August (which is not uncommon), you could shift into giving workshops and retreats during those times. You could also move clients, if they were willing, from one of your services to another at appropriate times, for example, from spiritual direction into one of your workshops or retreats or groups, and back again.

It is a good idea to try to develop a new source of income each year—some new group or workshop you add to your menu of services. You could then keep track of the amount of income it generates, the expenses associated with it, the time you invested in it, and then re-evaluate it at the end of the year, primarily taking into account how much or how little your clients seemed to benefit from it. Make sure you let your clients know about your new services.

The more choice you give your clients the better. Freedom of choice, the ability to make your own custom-designed spiritual growth program, is an important feature to offer people.

Ongoing Training

In general, get all the training and education you can in every aspect of spiritual direction, because every year there are more and more spiritual directors and more and more masters and doctoral degree programs being offered in spiritual direction. The whole field is becoming increasingly professional, so if you don't keep up-to-date through constant training, in five or ten years you won't be able to keep up. Consider spending at least five to ten percent of your gross income per year on ongoing training. Besides just keeping up, this can be very stimulating for you.

Positive Termination And Referral

To keep your practice stable and growing, positive termination is absolutely essential. This is because when a client quits, their last impression is the most important one. The final impression you make on a client is as important, or more important, than the first one. Last impressions are lasting impressions. Former clients will think of this impression when they are thinking about returning to you themselves, or when they think of referring others to you.

When a client terminates, act towards them out of an abundance mentality, as if you had a long waiting list of new clients you could call upon to fill the gap left by this terminating one.

Also, ask them to let others know that you now have an opening and to refer others to you. They will usually be happy to do this, as it will alleviate any guilt they may feel about terminating.

Whatever you do, don't shame, blame, or guilt them for terminating. Keep any fear, depression, and exasperation on your part under tight lock and key. This will be hard if you particularly valued this client, and also because you have just lost part of your income.

I once saw a therapist for a particular problem I was dealing with. After a few sessions I decided I really couldn't afford his high fee. When I told him I was quitting his whole demeanor changed from being very compassionate to very aggressive. He began to berate me and tell me how badly I needed therapy and how I would never be able to work through this problem on my own. He also had the nerve to tell me what *I* was feeling! He told me that I was just thinking of quitting because I was depressed, which was not true at all. That was my last session with him and I will certainly never refer anyone to him for therapy.

It is a good idea, when a new person begins spiritual direction, to tell them up front or in your office policy handout that you believe in positive termination. Ask them to give you advance notice so you can prepare to do a final closure session with them.

When someone terminates with me, in the closure session I (tactfully) read back to them my notes, starting at our first session, and ask for their comments. This is usually an interesting trip down memory lane for them, and lets them see their progress. Then we fill out a Spiritual Direction Evaluation form together.

In my experience, if you let them fill out the evaluation form at home, few evaluations will come back to you, but the ones that do will be more completely filled out and more honest than the ones done in person. So, it's a tradeoff.

Make sure you correct any areas of your practice they think need improving. One client pointed out to me that I had a particular way of saying "Hhhhmmm" that sounded like a judgement to her. I have been careful about how I say "Hhhmmm" ever since. Another said that she "honestly didn't give a damn about her Myers-Briggs type" so I have been very cautious from then on about just assuming people will be interested in this. It reminded me to separate out my interests from what the client really needs. Honest feedback can be very humbling and also very useful.

The basic elements of spiritual direction evaluation are: where were they with their spiritual issues when they started, where are they now, and what future areas might they want to work on with you or someone else?

Outline a plan of things they could work on with you if they stayed or came back in the future, and let them know you are totally okay if they still decide to quit now. Throughout the evaluation, discuss the client's progress, what they got out of spiritual direction, what they wanted to get out of it but failed to get, and so on.

At the end tell the client what the sessions meant to you, how you enjoyed working with them, and give them feedback on anything you can honestly praise them for. For example, "I've really appreciated what an upbeat person you are." Or "I like how serious you are about your spiritual quest." The clients will leave on a positive note, feeling complete and happy. If you let clients go graciously they may come back later themselves or they may refer others to you.

Clients coming back six months or a year later has happened many times for me, and other spiritual directors report that this also happens with their clients.

Now that you have lost a client, you need to trust your Higher Power to provide a new one, and it is up to you to take positive action to bring this about. In my experience, action is one of the best cures for anxiety.

In some cases you may be the one to initiate termination. Again, operate out of abundance and always keep the client's best interests in mind. If they are not the right type of client for you, or if you believe another spiritual director could serve them better, refer them to that person. That spiritual director may refer other people to you.

An alternative would be to refer a client to a psychologist or other therapist while you continue to do spiritual direction with them. As mentioned earlier, if you are referring someone, it is best to contact the person you are referring them to first, to see if they are taking new clients and to ensure it would be a good match. Then let your client know that they can continue to see you while they also see the therapist.

Keeping In Touch

It's important to treat all clients, active or inactive, as if they were in a permanent relationship with you. Keep in contact with all previous clients through emailing or mailing them newsletters, or through phoning them just to see how they are doing. If you phone them you do not need to bring up the possibility of them returning to spiritual direction with you—they will bring it up themselves, positively or negatively. They may not be interested in returning themselves, but your email, mail, or phone call will keep you in their mind, and they may refer someone else to you.

Start Your Own Center

If you made a list of all the spiritual directors and counselors, and spiritually-oriented therapists, social workers, psychologists, life coaches, and practitioners of alternate healing in your local area, you might be able to get together with them and start your own Spirituality and Personal Growth Center. Together you could share space for offices, workshops, and groups, do a joint newsletter, and so on. If there is nothing like this in your area, it might fill a huge need. And there is always great power in numbers and cross-fertilization of ideas and mutual support.

For Full-Time
Spiritual Directors and Counselors

CHAPTER TEN

The Reality of Developing a Full-Time Spiritual Direction Practice—It's Tough!

Positive Reasons To Be A Full-Time Spiritual Director

Being a part-time spiritual director or counselor has great rewards, but being a full-time one can be even more exhilarating and rewarding. Now you can more fully serve your Higher Power, more completely fulfill your vocation of being a spiritual guide, and drink more deeply from the well of joy of being a vital part of the spiritual growth of others.

As well, the freedom of being your own boss and following your own agenda rather than that of some corporate entity, be it a church or other institution, can be truly liberating. The decisions about what must be done are no longer imposed on you through a hierarchical system, they now rest squarely on your shoulders, for better or for worse.

You can be as creative as you want to be, and the possibilities are virtually unlimited.

When you are working full-time as a spiritual guide you get to design your own job, and you can make it any way you want it to be.

The Reality Of Being A Full-Time Spiritual Director: It's Tough

The good news about being on your own is that it can be great fun and an adventure. The bad news is that developing and maintaining a sizable number of clients can be very tough.

What I am about to tell you about the difficulty of being a full-time spiritual guide is not meant in any way to discourage you from pursuing this. Just the opposite. My intent in sharing the reality of it is so that you will understand why so few people who feel called to be a spiritual guide actually end up working full-time in that capacity. This will prepare you well to avoid common pitfalls and increase the chances that you will succeed in your own spiritual guidance practice.

If you know in advance what you are getting into, you will be much better prepared to cope with it. One of the parables of Jesus is about the wise king who counted the cost before he decided to go to war. So, because I sincerely want you to succeed, I am recommending that you seriously count the cost before you launch into a full-time practice.

The President of the Coordinating Council of Spiritual Directors International estimated in 2001 that two thirds of those who complete spiritual director training do not become full-time spiritual directors. Given my experience and observations, I would estimate that it is more like ninety to ninety-five percent.

Usually people do spiritual direction part-time. Their main job is teaching, parenting, being a counselor, administrator, psychologist, social worker, priest, minister, or religious educator. In fact, you will probably need to do some other job at least part-time in order to provide you with some steady income while you are building your practice.

The very first thing you need to understand in building a full-time spiritual guidance practice is that it will probably take you three to five years before you start getting enough regular referrals to begin to feel somewhat secure in your work. Since I was working full-time at another job and building my spiritual direction practice on a part-time basis on the side, it only took me three years after I went full-time as a spiritual director to reach the point of feeling secure. If you don't have a part-time practice already up and running before you go full-time, expect it to take five years.

On the other hand, I didn't have a book written for spiritual counselors like this one to guide me when I started out and had to learn a lot of things the hard way. So with the help of this book you may be able to develop your practice a lot faster. For now though, don't quit your day job. Build your practice on the side until you have enough directees to enable you to jump to doing spiritual direction full-time.

The second thing you need to understand is that, once you become a full-time spiritual guide, you will have no steady income to rely on. You will no longer have the comfort of knowing that you will get a nice pay check every two weeks whether you worked hard during those two weeks or not. Running a full-time spiritual counseling practice is not like an Employee Assistance Program where a big agency refers a steady stream of people to you and the client doesn't pay you, rather the EAP covers your salary and expenses. When you are on your own, the only time you get paid is when you see clients. If you don't see clients, you don't get paid. When I started out as a spiritual director, I had many days when I saw no clients at all, and I still have occasional days like that. So, be prepared for days of no income, and be prepared for low income.

In 1997 I visited a man who was a bit of a legend in my city. Gord had been the Provincial (director) of his religious order in Ontario but had fallen in love and left the order to get married. When I met him he seemed to be doing quite well at running his private practice. He was doing grief counseling with many people, doing "Healing Your Inner Child" workshops everywhere, and everyone loved him.

When I asked him what the secret of his success was, he said two things: "building relationships" and "not being uptight about having a low income." When I asked him to define "low-income" he said that, after three years of being in full-time practice, and after subtracting income taxes and business expenses, he was making about $15,000 a year.

Gord was a bright man and worked hard at his practice, was well-known, popular, and respected, but his income was low for someone with a master's degree in counseling. In terms of 2011 in Canada, his net income then was equivalent to about $30,000 per year now.

When you are on your own and not working for a company or institution, you also have no benefits package unless you purchase one privately. In other words, you have no medical, dental, short term disability or long term disability coverage. As well, there is no employment insurance provided by the government to those who are self-employed.

It obviously helps immensely, if you have a family, to be married to a spouse who has a good family benefits package as part of their work contract. If you were on your own, with no spouse or children, you could survive full-time in this work, but if you were the only bread-winner in your family, it would be extremely challenging.

You also have to remember that there are no longer any paid vacations or paid statutory holidays. Since I had always enjoyed this major benefit in my previous jobs, it took about a year for it to dawn on me that "Hey! When I am on a vacation or enjoying Christmas Day or New Years Day, I am *not* getting paid for it." What a revelation!

Another major adjustment is not having an expense account. On previous jobs there was always a certain amount of discretionary money to cover the purchase of needed, job-related expenses. When you are on your own, that money comes out of *your* pocket. The cost of photocopying, office supplies, postage, etc. is subtracted from your income. (On a positive note, these "business write-offs" can lower your income taxes—more about that later.)

Getting a spiritual counseling practice up and running is like rocket launching: because of inertia, two-thirds of the energy is spent in getting the rocket off the ground. However, once it is on its way and "breaks the surly bonds of earth," it takes very little energy to keep it going. When you have about forty clients, the practice seems to take on a life of its own and starts to run itself. The problem lies in surviving long enough to get to that point.

As a spiritual guide, you need to be prepared to put a lot of extra energy into the front end of your practice. You will have to work long and hard for two or three years to get it off the launching pad. It will be very slow at first because you will be spending most of your time on promoting your practice, that is, letting people know you are out there. However, once launched it will start to become self-perpetuating and be less demanding on you.

Establishing a spiritual counseling practice is also like riding a roller coaster. You have to be flexible and adapt to the client. So be prepared for clients rescheduling their appointments with you. Be prepared for clients not showing up for appointments and wanting to take December and the summer off. Be prepared for clients starting and then quitting a few sessions later. Be prepared for thinking you are going to see ten clients this week and suddenly being down to five.

In my own practice, my schedule can still be quite chaotic every now and then even after nine full-time years at it. As I write this, three of my four appointments today called to reschedule because of the weather—we are having a snowstorm. I also quickly learned that I would have to be prepared to work a lot of evenings and Saturdays, because that is when people are available. I am trying to work within set days and hours each week, but because I don't know in advance my clients' schedules, I still try to remain as flexible as possible. I keep all day Sunday and Monday, as well as Friday and Saturday nights free for my family and usually take one morning around midweek off for self-care, but the rest of my schedule is negotiable, which means I write in the mornings and then see clients afternoons, evenings, and Saturdays during the day. Sometimes I see clients Monday night or all day Monday if I am taking the following Saturday off.

So, welcome to rocket launching, roller coaster riding, a chaotic schedule, and welcome to your new boss, the client. You may have thought you were going to escape having a boss through setting up your own practice, but basically each of your clients is now your boss.

Like most human beings, your client's radio will most often be tuned to WIIFM, that is, What's In It For Me? Fortunately or unfortunately, that is the way the human creature is built. You may have been under the illusion that, now that you have a certificate or bachelor's, master's, or doctoral degree in spiritual direction, clients would flock to you in appreciation of all the work you put in to get qualified at this. Not so.

Most clients will not really care about your qualifications to do this type of work. They will judge everything by only one criteria: what am I getting out of this? If they believe they are getting a lot, they will continue. If they feel they are not getting much, they will fire you by quitting.

There are also a number of built-in problems with being a full-time spiritual counselor that you have to face. First of all you must have a high threshold for listening to people tell you their problems all day. If you don't take care of yourself, you may absorb a lot of their negativity, stress, depression, and loneliness. (I will discuss how to combat these things towards the end of the book.) I take a self-care Thursday morning each week and either have a session with my own spiritual director or therapist, or do a lot of journaling, or just do some fun thing like updating my iPod's podcasts or downloading music. I used to work from Tuesday morning to Friday night without a break, but it just got to be too much.

With spiritual direction, there is the problem of it being such a well-kept secret, so that the vast majority of people—even among those who go to church—have never heard of it. If people do know about spiritual direction, they often still believe that it is only by and for the ordained. That is, they believe only priests and ministers and religious offer it as a service, and only priests, ministers, and religious partake of it. They can't imagine a lay person as a spiritual director or directee. Fortunately, this is beginning to change.

As well, many spiritual directors experience a problem with the name itself. If you call yourself a "spiritual counselor" or "spiritual companion" or "spiritual friend" it sounds too New Agey for some church-goers. On the other hand, "spiritual director" sounds like you direct peoples' lives and tell them what to do, which people in our individualistic society resist. Many people also have the misconception that spiritual direction is therapy.

There are ways of coping with all of the above problems with establishing a full-time spiritual guidance practice, which we will look at later, but again, I am letting you know some of the more obvious difficulties now, not to discourage you, but so that you will go into this with your eyes wide open and prepare yourself to deal effectively with these problems.

Otherwise, you might find, as so many potential spiritual counselors have found in the past, that developing a spiritual guidance practice is a very difficult thing to do, and quit after six months or a year. Again, my whole purpose in writing this book is to help you succeed rather than fail at this vital and holy service to others.

CHAPTER ELEVEN

It's Tough...But Your
Higher Power is There to Help You

Given all the difficulties of developing this type of practice, I can understand why there are so few people working as full-time spiritual counselors.

While it *is* tough, there is one overpowering beacon of light in the midst of the darkness, that is, the unexpected providence of your Higher Power.

Developing this practice is an opportunity to grow in the faith that, when you need your Higher Power the most, your Higher Power will be there for you. When you hit rock bottom, you have two basic choices: to either quit or to trust in a deeper way that your Higher Power will pull you through.

There are two main mistakes we make when it comes to relying upon our Higher Power. The first mistake is to think that we have to do it all, and our Higher Power is not going to do anything. This is similar to the "God helps those who help themselves" attitude that pervades our culture, which in effect makes God irrelevant.

The second mistake is the opposite of the first: to believe that our Higher Power will do everything and we don't have to do anything.

The solution to both these mistakes is to recognize that the Higher Power specializes in the impossible. The Higher Power normally refuses to do what is humanly possible. Why would our Higher

Power do something that is humanly possible, if we don't care enough to do it ourselves? If we don't care about it, why would our Higher Power?

On the other hand, if we do care about it, and do what is ours to do, then the Higher Power is more than willing to step in and do the impossible, multiplying our efforts in unpredictable ways.

Twenty years ago, at the Canadian Theological Students Conference in Ottawa, I happened to be standing in the lineup for lunch in front of Adam Exner, Archbishop of the Archdiocese of Winnipeg. When he learned I came from Winnipeg too, he invited me to have lunch with him. Over lunch I asked him if he ever felt overwhelmed in his role as archbishop. This humble servant of God confided "I feel overwhelmed all the time, but I just keep offering the Lord my little loaves and fishes, and he keeps on multiplying them."

In 1998, when I first felt the call to be a spiritual director, I decided I had better get a little training in how to do spiritual direction. I thought maybe a weekend workshop would be enough to get me started. I realize now how hopelessly naive I was then. However, I started to inquire about training in spiritual direction, everything just started falling miraculously into place, and within a few months I found myself in a Doctor of Ministry in Spiritual Direction program, scarcely knowing how I got there.

At one point, I realized I would need a thesis supervisor, and I had no idea who in the world I could get to do this. Surely no one in my little city of London, Ontario would have a Doctor of Ministry in Spiritual Direction and also be able to meet all of the other criteria for thesis supervisors stipulated by the doctoral program.

A little while later I was at a farewell party for a colleague. There were some Sisters of St. Joseph there, and one of them, whom I hardly knew, for some reason came over and started talking to me. We quickly discovered that she not only had a Doctor of Ministry degree in Spiritual Direction, but it was from the Graduate Theological Foundation in Indiana, the same school where I was doing my doctorate! Also, since she was a professor at a seminary, she would qualify to be my thesis supervisor. When I asked if she was interested in helping me out, she said yes, and Margaret Ferris,

CSJ, turned out to be the perfect supervisor for my thesis.

The Higher Power works in mysterious ways. You will find that clients, opportunities, and money come to you in strange ways. For example, I once put my brochures out in the local parishes, someone for some reason took my brochures from his or her parish to a conference in a city two hundred miles away, and some people from that city contacted me and became some of my most long-term clients.

Another example of how the seed grows, we know not how, occurred when I introduced my son Brandon to the Enneagram. Brandon told his best friend Jonathon about it, and Jonathon got his father interested in it. Jonathon's father was the principal of St. Theresa school, and one day asked the staff if they knew anyone he could contact to give the staff a workshop on the Enneagram for their annual Day of Prayer. One of my directees happened to be working at the school that day as a supply teacher and gave him my name. Jonathon's father then called me and we set up the workshop, totally oblivious to the fact that our sons were each other's best friend, and Jonathan's father had become interested in the Enneagram through Jonathon, through Brandon, through me! When we found out all this on the day of the workshop, we had a good laugh about the strange ways the Higher Power works.

One of the more dramatic examples of the Higher Power's care and providence happened like this. A lady in great distress came to me for spiritual direction and I quickly discerned that she had no money to pay for it, so I decided to do spiritual direction with her for free, because she so obviously needed it. She seemed to be coming apart at the seams.

Late one day, I was listening to her vent her hatred for her husband as usual, and after an hour, had absorbed a lot of her negative energy and turmoil. I tossed and turned in my bed that night. When I arose (I didn't wake since I hadn't slept) I felt horrible. I was really struggling with my whole spiritual direction practice at that point since I was barely surviving financially at it, and I felt so bad that I wondered if I shouldn't just call it quits.

I got out my journal and decided to write a dialogue with Jesus about whether I should continue in this practice or not. I wrote down all the problems I was having getting this practice launched. I was about to write down what I thought Jesus's answer was, when at that very second the phone rang.

I answered the phone and it was someone asking me to give a Day of Prayer at St. Anne's school. I had contacted them many months ago and since there had been no response I had totally forgotten about them. But here they were calling me (at 7:30 in the morning) to come and do it.

I went back to writing. Jesus, I felt, was telling me not to worry about the money I needed to continue my practice, he would take care of it. The next day seventeen hundred and fifty dollars appeared in my mailbox!

Fifteen hundred was a gift from my mother for completing my doctorate. This was a total surprise. The other two hundred and fifty was an honorarium from the federal government awarded to Grace, my wife, for coming third in a nationwide essay contest on how to improve the Canadian health care system. The value of this prize was far more than the money awarded. Grace was looking for a better nursing job and this award would help her get it. Indeed she landed a much better job shortly thereafter.

Grace had entered the essay contest months ago, and since she received no response, she had totally forgotten about it, much as I had forgotten about St. Anne's school. The fact that, right at my lowest point, the school had called me out of the blue at such an unusual time of the day and right in the middle of my journaling about whether or not to quit my practice, and the next day two completely unexpected money gifts from totally different sources ended up in our mailbox on the same day, were undeniable signs to me that Jesus would indeed take care of the money for my practice, and therefore I should continue.

So, even though it is very difficult to get a full-time spiritual direction practice established, remember that your Higher Power is always with you, and "where God guides, God provides." If your Higher Power really called you to this, your Higher Power will provide the means for you to do it.

This brings us to a very important question: Are you really called to full-time spiritual direction or counseling?

CHAPTER TWELVE

Are You Called to be a Full-Time Spiritual Director?

Before you go any further, it is important to ask yourself: am I called to do spiritual guidance, direction or counseling as a full-time practice? If not, you are wasting your time, for to paraphrase scripture: "If you build without your Higher Power, you build in vain."

First of all, before pondering that question, you may be wondering if you are called to be a spiritual director or counselor at all. If this is the case, ask yourself the following:

How old are you? Richard Rohr, a well-respected retreat master and spiritual director, thinks that spiritual directors should be at least fifty. Before that age, very few people have any real depth of wisdom. On the other hand, Jesus was only thirty when he began his ministry, so age may not matter as much as maturity and spiritual depth. In general though, I think it could be said that a spiritual director should be at least thirty.

What life experiences have you had? This relates to the question of age as well. Have you lived long enough to be able to empathize with people who are struggling with their marriage or religious vocation, unemployment, physical or mental health problems, addictions of all kinds, atheism, the meaning of life, the loss of loved ones, dark nights of the soul, or problems with the church or organized religion in general? If you haven't had at least a few of these experiences, it is too early for you to be a spiritual director because you will not have any real spiritual depth.

Do people seek you out for counseling or spiritual direction? Assuming that you qualify to be a spiritual director or counselor, given the above criteria, and that you have been trained to be one, the next question is: how do I discern whether or not I am called to this *full-time*? To answer this, consider the following questions, (which could also be of further help to the person who is discerning if they have been called to be a spiritual director or counselor at all):

What are your options? Is being a full-time spiritual director the best way you can serve God? Before going any further, clearly describe all your options. Perhaps you are called to do spiritual direction part-time or even just a few hours a week or month. Perhaps you are not quite ready to do this full-time but you will be in the future. Are there other better ways you could serve your Higher Power right now? Once you have listed all your options, be willing to do whatever your Higher Power wants.

Can you afford this? Are you willing to work for low pay or reduced pay? Jesus said that a wise builder counts the cost before building. You need a part-time job or enough back-up money to help you get through the first few years at least.

Have you prayed a lot about this decision to be a full-time spiritual director? Have you asked others to pray that you make a good discernment?

Have you consulted with your own spiritual director about this, and what is he or she saying?

What is your head, heart, and gut saying to you about doing this full-time? Have you listed and weighed all the pros and cons of doing this, using your God-given intellect? Just listing the pros and cons and adding them up is not enough because one pro can carry more weight than ten cons, or vice versa. You need to consider not just how many pros and cons there are, but also how important each one is to you. Do you have feelings of consolation (affective movements of peace, happiness, love) when you contemplate this move, or feelings of desolation (affective movements of doubt or anxiety)? Also, what are your deep intuition and gut instincts saying to you about this?

Do you feel drawn to this or driven to it? The Higher Power draws us to things rather than forcing them on us. The Spirit works by way of invitation not force. Do you feel freedom or compulsion when you contemplate this? If you feel driven, it is probably fueled by your ego not your Higher Power.

What would your scriptures or any person whose spiritual judgement you trust say about it?

What would the person or persons who hold legitimate authority in your life say about this decision? Would your bishop, superior, or boss think this was a good idea? Is your spouse or life partner and your family supportive and encouraging you in this decision?

Have there been any outward signs of what you should do? Are you being objective about these signs or just reading what you want into them? A farm boy, who wanted to get off the farm, was helping his father with the planting one day when he noticed some clouds that looked like the letters "P" and "C". He said to his father "Look father, the heavens are telling me to 'preach Christ'." His father, who wanted him to stay on the farm with him, smiled and said "No, no, you've got it all wrong son. The heavens are telling you to 'plant corn'."

Also, remember that, just because you have not received any outward signs, does not mean that you should or should not pursue this. Sometimes signs are there, sometimes they are not.

If all of the above considerations point in the same direction, then this is probably your Higher Power's will for you, and you should resolutely pursue it. Running into obstacles, or not receiving signs, does not mean you made the wrong choice. It is normal to encounter obstacles when pursuing anything worthwhile. However, if some of the above considerations point in one direction, and others point in different directions, it means that you should keep praying, discerning, consulting trusted advisors, and waiting until your path of action becomes clear.

CHAPTER THIRTEEN

Spiritual and Emotional Support

Your foundational support in this work will come from your Higher Power. If you build the house without the Foundation, the house will surely fall, sooner or later.

Therefore, it is essential that you keep your spiritual life alive and well. Keep the lines of communication open with your Higher Power through prayer. I start the day with contemplative prayer, verbal prayer, meditation, and spiritual reading that keeps my spiritual heart pumping. As I begin work, I pray specifically for my practice: for wisdom, guidance, and discernment in every aspect of it. I believe this is the lifeblood of my practice.

When I feel discouraged, I find it helpful to count my blessings and all of my Higher Power's providence in my work. I make lists of all the ways my Higher Power has helped me so far, and this usually cheers me up and gives me renewed confidence. When I review my "blessings lists," I feel totally supported and blessed. I also remind myself that many of my clients have said they would pray for me, and I sense their support.

Beyond your Higher Power, your next line of support is your own self-care. Running a spiritual guidance practice can be stressful, lonely, and energy-draining unless you take action to protect and support yourself. It is crucial to humbly acknowledge your limits, to know when to say no to well-intentioned requests from others, to take daily rest breaks (or coffee), to exercise regularly, and to take holidays yearly or even every three or four months, because the tendency when you are launching a practice is to never stop working.

When you work for others, as most people do, constantly doing the agenda of the business or institution you are working for, not your own agenda, it is natural to want to take all the breaks you are allowed. However, when you work for yourself, it is easy to overwork. Since you don't have a steady paycheck coming in every two weeks, and you never know if it's going to be feast or famine in the months ahead, and everything you earn is based on your constant effort, it can be tempting to ignore your physical needs.

At first I worked twelve hour days, only pausing for 15 minutes to eat. Now, in addition to taking an hour for lunch and dinner, I take poetry, astronomy, and centering prayer breaks in order to temporarily take my mind off my work so that I can return to it twenty minutes later in a refreshed mood. I believe this makes me more productive and creative in the long run.

If you are in a relationship, the next key support would be from your partner. If you are married it is crucial that you have your spouse's support, understanding, and patience for this demanding work. If you take care of your loved ones, they will usually support and take care of you. Therefore, it is a good idea to block off a certain amount of time, maybe an hour or more each day, to spend with them.

It is important to make this time with your loved ones non-negotiable with your clients. In other words, this time is sacrosanct. You must absolutely refuse to see clients during this time and suggest they find another spiritual counselor if the only time they can see you is during your blocked off "loved ones time." If you don't do this, the urgent needs and ever-varying schedules of your clients, and your own need for income, can pressure you to sacrifice this sacred time. If you are really stressed about your family finances, you may need to take a part-time job.

To counteract the isolation of running a private practice, you may also need to develop your friendships and social life more. You may need the support of a supervisor or even psychological support in the form of therapy to counter the negative emotions you absorb from your clients. Spiritual counseling can also be very sedentary, you are sitting all day, so a solid exercise program can counteract the tendency to neglect our bodies.

It is necessary to do all of the above things to maintain your spiritual, psychological, emotional, physical, social, marital, and relational health. Running a full-time spiritual counseling practice can be taxing in all these areas of your life.

Every spiritual director should have their own spiritual director and work out arrangements for individual or group peer supervision. You could benefit as well from having a spiritual directors' peer support group whom you handpick to be supportive. You could invite them over for lunch or dinner and then pray together and share how you each experience doing this work.

CHAPTER FOURTEEN

Basic Attitudes for Full-Time Spiritual Direction

Spirituality can be involved in anything, including a business. Since as a spiritual director, your main concern is helping others as well as yourself draw closer to the Higher Power, it is essential that you integrate running your small business/spiritual direction practice into your spiritual rule or spiritual discipline. Running this small business can be an important part of your spiritual path and your spiritual growth. Running your practice can be a powerful way to connect to your Higher Power.

Since it is your Higher Power who builds your practice, not you, the main requirement on your part is to surrender to your Higher Power. You have to get your ego out of the way, let go, and let your Higher Power lead you. This takes a great deal of trust, and is a real opportunity for growth in faith.

Most of the time, my schedule is full of appointments for the next two weeks, but beyond that it usually looks pretty sketchy. I find I have to keep moving forward, trusting that my Higher Power will fill up the void as I approach it. My Higher Power usually does this, but also keeps me in a place where I have to rely upon my Higher Power to provide me with my next meal beyond two weeks down the road.

Now I know something of how the Israelites felt when they wandered in the desert. God provided them with fresh manna every day (Exodus 16:31-35). If they tried to store up two days worth at a time, it went rotten so they couldn't eat it. They had to live in holy insecurity, and so do I, trusting for me and my family that God will "give us this day our daily bread."

In one of the Indiana Jones movies the hero is faced at one point with a large chasm that he has to somehow get across in order to get the Holy Grail on the other side. Legend has it that there is a glass bridge across the chasm, but you cannot see it until you take the first step, and many men have plummeted to their death. That seems to be my situation most of the time. I keep taking that first step and my Higher Power keeps being the glass bridge beneath my feet.

Someone said that:

"When you have gone to the edge
of all the light you know
And you are about to step off
into the darkness of the unknown
Faith is knowing
one of two things will happen:
either there will be
something solid to stand on
or you will learn how to fly."

This is faith. This is an accurate description of developing a full-time spiritual direction practice.

So far my Higher Power has not asked me to learn how to fly, except on the wings of prayers, those of myself and others. I am sure it is the prayers of others that have sustained me more than my own prayers, but running a spiritual direction practice requires you to be very prayerful.

The main attitude in running a spiritual direction practice is that of living the gospel.

When we put God and love and non-egotistical, detached service first, when we put God's righteousness/ethics first, when we put people before profits, and when we walk our talk, word will get around that we are a person of integrity, a wise and just spiritual role model/mentor, and our practice will thrive.

You will also need the attitude of persistence. Persevering and never giving up regardless of the adversity you face is not easy. As I wrote earlier, this work can be very discouraging. In any field, people often give up when they don't get immediate results.

I find it helps to have a motivation and accountability system. First, I set measurable, achievable goals and a deadline. To keep myself accountable to those goals, I review my progress toward them once a week. When I achieve a goal, I reward myself with something meaningful to me, for example, going to a movie or out for coffee with a friend. Meaningful rewards are simple things that can motivate us to keep fighting the good fight. I worked for several years in the field of behavior management and I know that rewarding yourself for goals achieved is a basic self-motivation strategy.

Another attitude is to think positively. I find that I have to give myself pep talks during the down times, to focus on the things I have done right rather than what I have done wrong, and to realize that, yes, I have done some stupid, clumsy things but in general I have done more things right than wrong.

The Higher Power is generous by nature and by grace, and an attitude of gratitude on our part can work wonders. Continually counting our blessings rather than our woes, and praising our Higher Power for those blessings, either pleases our Higher Power and somehow causes our Higher Power to be even more generous to us, or it conditions our minds and emotions to look for and expect blessings, which results in even more blessings flowing to us. This is the universal "Law of Attraction," that is, "What you focus on grows."

Some people use positive personal affirmations to try to overcome negative thinking, for example, "I am an excellent spiritual director." Perhaps it is part of fallen human nature, but the tendency for many people is to immediately think of a negative response like "No I'm not, I hardly have any clients." A way to overcome this is to write down your affirmation, write beside it any negative responses that come up, and then write beside each negative response a positive counter-affirmation such as "Yes, I don't have many clients right now, but I will have lots in the near future." With prayer and persistent affirmations, our Inner Critic will eventually give up. To paraphrase Ignatius of Loyola: "Rebuke your Inner Critic (the devil), and your Inner Critic (the devil) will flee from you." At the same time, you have to have an attitude of realism and honesty towards yourself. Maybe you are doing things that are driving clients away that no amount of prayer and affirmations will overcome, until you change your ways.

Another barrier to running a full-time spiritual direction practice can be negative feelings about money. I find it helps to remember that money itself is morally neutral. It is excessive love of money that is the problem. As Jesus and Gandhi said, the only devils in the world are those inside our own hearts. Greed is the problem, not money.

God does not want us to have too much money, so that we live in luxury while others starve. Nor does God want us to have too little money, so that we are tempted to manipulate people in order to get money, and so hurt others and ourselves.

Another helpful attitude is to keep in mind that if your practice goes well financially, everyone will benefit. If you are wise, you will save ten percent of your earnings so you will have a cushion for slow times, so your practice can continue. This will help you feel more relaxed and freer and thus do spiritual counseling better. You will be less worried, happier, more welcoming, and less tempted to manipulate people. You will be able to afford more training and be able to use the things you learn to expand the services you offer. You will be able to buy more books and audio-visual materials your clients can borrow for free. Your clients will benefit greatly from all of this.

A very important attitude I have learned is to turn problems and obstacles into opportunities. For example, when I had a day with no appointments, or when a client failed to show up, or a client phoned at the last minute to reschedule (this can happen often), I used to feel depressed and full of self-doubt and criticism. Now I just think "Thank you God for this freed-up time. I believe you purposely opened up this time for me so that I can serve you even more effectively. So, what can I do right now that has the greatest potential for bringing more clients to me in the future?" Thus there is no longer any wasted, "down time" in which I mope around wondering what I am doing wrong.

An example of this happened recently. A client who I really enjoy working with did not show up for her appointment. I was already feeling vulnerable at the time, and this no-show could have precipitated a lot of self-doubt. However, I decided to make lemonade from this lemon and used the time to email about four hundred people my another installment of "Top Ten Spiritual Growth Ideas." As a result of this I received some positive feedback and a referral for a new client. (Again, I think "spam" is okay if used judiciously and sparingly—say once or twice a month maximum—and you have something of genuine spiritual value to offer people.)

When I phoned my absentee client to see why she had missed the session, she was very apologetic. She didn't show up because it was Halloween and she got so wrapped up in the fun she was having decorating her house that our appointment completely slipped her mind. We rescheduled right away, and everything was fine.

I was doubly relieved since she had a good excuse and I had not squandered my time beating myself up over her absence. As it turned out her absence had nothing to do with anything I had done anyway. You will find that a client's absence usually has more to do with them and what is going on in their life than with anything you have done wrong.

It is also important to have an attitude of abundance, not scarcity. Scarcity can make you competitive, abundance can make you generous. If you believe there are enough clients out there for everybody, you lighten up and loosen up, and think about how you can help other spiritual counselors find clients. On the other hand, if you think there is a limited pool of clients, you will want to compete with other counselors, and limit their access to the pool.

An abundance mentality comes from believing in God's overflowing love and that God has given all of us abundant resources of energy, time, contacts, clients, and money. Money is only a small part of abundance and is just paper or metal that is designated as legal tender. Focusing on getting more money is not going to give you sustained motivation. Money follows focusing on abundance, not vice versa. In other words, focusing on money may bring you paper and metal, but it does not bring true abundance. Serving others and making a difference in the world motivates most successful entrepreneurs more than money.

Someone said that "When you are up to your neck in alligators, it's easy to forget that your original goal was to drain the swamp." Similarly, if you focus too much on money matters in running your spiritual counseling practice, it is easy to forget that your original goal and motivation was to help others grow spiritually. Therefore, some good things to remind yourself of every now and then are "I am doing all this because I care about people," and "This is a service, or a ministry first of all, not a business" and "I am not in this to get rich, I am in this to help bring in the reign of God" and "The Lord is my Shepherd, I shall not want."

Another attitude is to be action-oriented. All the ideas I am giving you in this book will not do you one bit of good if you don't act on them. There are all kinds of subtle things that we learn when we take action. There is a big difference between reading about how to play basketball or drive a car, and actually doing it. Any "how to" book can just give you the rules and guidelines. On the other hand, you wouldn't be able to proceed properly without the manual.

When you start out, you need to be flexible not only with your time but also with the clients you take on. I decided right at the start of my practice that I would be open to taking anyone (unless they were mentally or emotionally unstable, in which case I would refer them to a professional therapist). I have had some clients who could only be described as "curmudgeonly" or even "disgusting." This has been challenging, but rewarding. I think I have learned more from my difficult clients than from the easier ones. It forces you to get your ego and your judgements out of the way, to be extremely tolerant, and to love everyone.

There is a lot of talk in spiritual direction about there needing to be a good "fit" between the spiritual director and the directee. My take on this is: the director/directee relationship either has to be a good "match," or you need to change yourself so that you can accept anyone. Saint Paul said he had learned to be "all things to all people." In other words, he learned to adapt to whatever the other person's needs were, without compromising his integrity. In my judgement, this also applies to spiritual directors.

This may seem to contradict what I said previously about a client's absence or quitting "usually has more to do with them and what is going on in their life than with anything you have done wrong," but another important attitude to adopt is the "One Hundred Percent Responsibility" rule. This means that if someone quits, you take 100% responsibility for this. You do not make excuses such as "This client was not committed enough." The reason for taking this attitude is that if you start making excuses or just blame the client for quitting, you will never look at what *you* may be doing to cause people to quit, and so you will never grow. But again, don't beat yourself up *too much* if someone doesn't show up or quits. Keep a healthy balance between being responsible for what you can control (your attitude and things you do) and what is out of your control (circumstances in your clients' lives).

When I talked to many spiritual directors who had difficulty getting or keeping clients, most had concluded that the problem was that "people don't make their spiritual life a priority" or "spirituality is not that important to people." Personally, I have found that most people *are* intensely interested in spirituality. This attitude prevented these directors from facing the fact that they may have been ineffectively approaching potential clients, or doing things to turn them off once they started. Blaming the clients let those directors off the hook of the difficult work of having to look at themselves

It takes an attitude of courage to risk rejection by phoning people, meeting people in networking, and doing workshops. Things seem to come and go in sets of three. Sometimes you gain three new clients one week and then lose three long-term clients the next week. You may feel, as Frank Sinatra sang in "That's Life," you were "riding high in April, shot down in May." It is easy to become discouraged, that is, to lose your courage. You can start to fear that you are going to lose all your clients, that you have been deluding yourself that you were called by your Higher Power to do this work, and start thinking seriously about getting out and trying something else. Whenever this fear strikes me, I take action by:

- writing down all the good, smart things I have done
- reminding myself that my clients are not all going to quit at the same time

- reminding myself that my Higher Power is in charge, and this is really my Higher Power's work, and that if my Higher Power wants it to happen, it will happen. If my Higher Power doesn't want it to happen, my Higher Power will provide something else for me.

Some final attitudes that will help you to not just survive but thrive as a spiritual director:

- expecting a lot from yourself and others, reaching out to give your personal best, striving for excellence.
- a willingness to work hard during times when there is no money. Some days you will earn a lot and other days you will earn nothing. Some years will be "boom" years and other years will be "bust" years. It is important to keep busy during the slow times.
- a willingness to do "pro bono" work, that is, to donate free of charge a certain percentage of your work with people who really cannot afford it.

CHAPTER FIFTEEN

Basic Skills for Full-Time Spiritual Direction

Basic Skills

The first basic skill in running your spiritual counseling practice as a small business is the ability to envision a mission statement and goals. As a spiritual guide, you will want to first of all choose a spiritual mission for your life, if you don't already have one. Your Higher Power knows you need money, food, and shelter and will take care of these things for you if you make your Higher Power your first priority. So you don't need to worry about your basic needs. A simple spiritual mission statement for your life might be "By the grace of God, I love God with my whole heart, and spread God's love to others."

Since you are operating a spiritual counseling practice, you are running a small business, and therefore you need a business mission, but it must be one that is compatible with the spiritual mission you have chosen for your life, as well as with your personal values. If your business mission is to get rich, and one of your personal values is to do spiritual direction with the poor, you will be driving with one foot on the gas and the other on the brake. Consequently, you will make a lot of noise, but go nowhere.

A good business mission has two parts: a vision and an action. The vision part is about the kind of world you want to create, and the action is what you are going to do to bring the vision about. For example, my business mission statement is "By the grace of God, I co-create a spiritual world by spiritual writing, teaching, and counseling." I know that I am not going to achieve this mission without my Higher Power's help, therefore I pray this mission statement every day and ask for God's help to do it.

A good business mission statement is lofty, something you could never achieve in one lifetime. You can break it down into smaller goals and objectives after you first formulate it. You may never achieve your mission fully, but you will achieve a lot more than you would if you didn't have a mission.

A second basic skill is time management. A little book that many people have found very helpful is Alan Lakein's *How to Get Control of Your Time and Life* (New American Library: New York, 1996). In it, Lakein says that to live well you have to know what your long term goals are for your life. If you know that, you can plan things every day or week that bring you one step closer to your life-goals. You can then block off time for those things in your weekly schedule so that you get the *important* things done and don't get caught up in always just taking care of what's *urgent*.

Lakein recommends planning and scheduling loosely. In other words, you create spaces in your schedule so that, if something urgent comes up that you cannot in good conscience ignore, you take care of it and then go back to your planned and important priorities. Loose scheduling is Lakein's happy-medium solution to two common time-management problems: to have no plans at all so you just drift through life, or to have plans that are so rigid and packed that you cannot take care of urgent matters when they arise.

So, the most basic task is to formulate a spiritual mission for your life and a business mission for your practice that is in line with your life's spiritual mission, and then to manage your time well around that business mission. Lakein advocates taking time to think about your work so that you work smarter, not harder, and so you work with ease. If you know you are working on your priority items you can just work at your own pace and still be much more effective than if you put terrific energy into non-priority items. Tremendous effort does not necessarily mean that you are accomplishing anything great.

Besides wise time management skills you need the ability to think positively. I have already mentioned the importance of having an "abundance mindset" to counteract your fears of not surviving financially. Positive thinking means you will be optimistic and resolute, both key qualities for survival in running a small business. Having an abundance mentality will also help you avoid hard-sell or "push" marketing in favor of soft-sell or "pull" marketing, which maintains your relational quality with your clients by relying on the power of attraction. In pull marketing, you believe that people are good, and they know that developing their spirituality is a good thing for them, so if you offer something that will obviously benefit them spiritually, they will be attracted to your services.

A fourth basic skill, besides mission formulation, effective time management, and positive thinking, is money management. I will be dealing with this in depth in later chapters, but for now suffice it to say that part of anyone's spiritual development is learning to handle money in a mature way, to neither ignore it nor make it your god.

Training and Staying Current

To be a spiritual director is first of all a calling and a gift from God. We must never lose sight of that. A person could have lots of training in spiritual direction, but if they have not been called or gifted, they won't bring about much transformation, that is, positive spiritual growth in their clients.

On the other hand, a person with no training but with a genuine calling and gift for spiritual direction could bring about great transformation, by the grace of God. On the other hand again, their results could be deeper and broader with a little training.

The best option would be for a person to not only be gifted and called, but also trained. The trained person will have much more knowledge of resources and methods for spiritual growth than those who are untrained.

Spiritual direction is becoming more and more professional. For example, there are now university degrees offered in spiritual direction at the masters and doctoral levels. There are more than four hundred centers training spiritual directors around the globe. There is an organization, Spiritual Directors International, that promotes spiritual direction on a world-wide basis. More and more people are taking training in spiritual direction, which means that the universities, colleges, and retreat centers that offer training can afford to be more selective in who they allow to enter the training.

As with other disciplines, as entrance requirements go up, and as people seek more and more training, standards will go up as to the amount of training you have to have in order to call yourself a spiritual director.

As someone wanting to be a full-time spiritual director, it would be wise for you to get all the training you can, because the more we equip ourselves, the better the service we are able to offer. Spiritual Directors International can put you in touch with all the training possibilities around the world and in your local area. See www.sdiworld.org.

If you are already well-trained, it is imperative that you stay current with the rapidly evolving and expanding field of spiritual direction. One of the best ways to do this is to subscribe to *Presence*, the premier journal in the field, published by Spiritual Directors International four times a year. Another way to stay current is to attend the annual conferences of Spiritual Directors International or your local organizing bodies who can also keep you up-to-date on new training opportunities and workshops in your area.

New books on spiritual direction are constantly being published and they are usually reviewed in *Presence*. Like any field, spiritual direction requires ongoing reading to keep on top of developments. It helps to block off an hour or two a week to do this reading, or to read at least a page of *Presence* each day you are working.

CHAPTER SIXTEEN

Nuts and Bolts of Developing a Full-Time Spiritual Direction Practice

The Biggest Barrier To
Becoming A Full-Time Spiritual Director

Let us acknowledge up front a big difficulty for spiritual directors in running their own private practice: in order to succeed at this, you have to be proficient both as a spiritual counselor and as a businessperson. You have to face the fact that a private practice is basically a small business, and it possesses the common features of all small businesses, things like budgeting, marketing, paper work, cash flow, and so on.

Here lies the crux of the problem and the reason why most spiritual counselors do not work full-time: most spiritual directors did not get into spiritual counseling because they wanted to run a business. They may be called to be a spiritual counselor but they may not be skilled at business. They got into this field because they wanted to love and serve their Higher Power in a deeper way, not because they loved business, administration, and technology.

Being a good spiritual counselor requires skills of prayer, listening, intuition, spiritual sensitivity, empathy, and insight, whereas the cultural stereotype is that being successful in business requires one to be calculating, subtly manipulative of your clients' desires, cold, hard, and only concerned with the bottom line. In other words, the stereotype of running a business is the exact opposite of what spiritual counseling requires.

My own previous idea of business, I must admit, was largely negative. I thought it was all about greed, competition, and dog-eat-dog survival. I found that if one is going to survive as a spiritual counselor running a small business, you first of all need a sound spiritual approach that allows you to let go of any negative stereotypes you have about business.

A good place to start is with the idea that everything in creation belongs to the Higher Power and is under the Higher Power's sovereignty, and this includes the world of business. The Higher Power, after all, is the creator and distributor of organizational and administrative gifts.

In my experience with spiritual directors, they tend to be blind to the fact that business is an inescapable part of everyone's life. Business produced the clothes you are wearing, the couch or chair you are sitting on, the dwelling you are in, the food you ate today, the car you drive, and this book.

God is everywhere, which means that God is in the center of just, ethical businesses and business practices as well. When Martin Luther, the great Protestant reformer, was asked if it was okay to sing exuberant songs in church he replied "Of course it is, why should the devil have all the good songs?" In our case we could ask "Is it okay to use marketing techniques to reach people with spiritual direction?" Luther would probably reply "Of course it is! Why should the devil have all the smart business practices?"

Billions of dollars are spent every year to entice people to consume, consume, consume. As spiritual counselors we need to learn how to market spiritual direction and counseling so that more people will pray, show mercy, do justice, and walk humbly with their God.

It has been a huge learning experience for me, since I started my spiritual direction practice, to discover that business can run on spiritual values and that operating your business well can make you a better, more relaxed, and more confident spiritual director. To be a good spiritual director and a good businessperson, you have to be "wise as a serpent and innocent as a dove." Being successful in business requires both wisdom and ethics.

Accountability To An Advisory Board

Running an independent spiritual counseling practice can bring a great sense of freedom. However, as any wise person knows, *too much* freedom can be a bad thing, and in this case it can make a spiritual counselor operating on their own vulnerable to the very real temptation to misuse their freedom by manipulating their clients.

I dealt with spiritual and emotional support in a previous chapter, but it is also necessary for a full-time spiritual counselor to have an ethical support system. It is imperative that you have your own spiritual director and supervisor or at least a peer supervision group whom you meet with regularly. It is also imperative that you have an advisory board. All of these people will help you maintain a high standard of ethics, which will make your practice thrive.

An advisory board is different than a peer supervision group. A peer supervision group, if it is functioning properly, focuses on what is going on inside you when you are doing spiritual direction. What attitudes or prejudices or insecurities in you, are preventing you from doing spiritual direction well? An advisory board consists of unpaid but professional people who know something about running a business, and about business ethics.

The advisory board does not have to be large. It could be composed of a spiritually-oriented business person, a technical-know-how person, someone who specializes in ethics in general or who is known to be a highly ethical person, and a spiritual director who knows the ethical implications of spiritual counseling well. As you meet with them and share what you have been doing maybe twice or four times a year, your advisory board will ensure that you are not inadvertently violating any ethical boundaries in the way you run your practice.

The advisory board can also be a great support for creative brainstorming on how to develop your practice, do a lot of networking for you with people they know, make you aware of new developments in technology you could use, and develop new referral sources for you.

What do they get out of it, if you are not paying them and they are donating their labor as volunteers? The same payback that any volunteer gets: the joy of helping others, except that in this case, they receive not only the joy of helping you but also joy in the knowledge that they are helping many other people spiritually through you.

The Practical Details Of Developing A Practice

Often, in training programs for spiritual directors, the participants engage in very creative things—they learn new ways of praying, they learn about the Enneagram, the writings of mystics and contemplatives, how to use clay, poetry, and painting in spiritual direction, and so on.

This all helps them to be creative spiritual directors, but none of this prepares them for the reality of actually operating a spiritual direction practice. I once saw a cartoon where a university student, still wearing his cap and gown after graduation, was clinging with all his might to the gates of the university and screaming "No, no, not the real world, not the real world!!" while his parents tried to drag him away.

There is a reason why seminaries often ask their students to do a year of practicum work with an actual parish or congregation before completing their final year of theology. These priests-to-be and ministers-to-be quickly learn that there is often a large disconnect between the ideals of being a student and the practical pastoral reality of running a church. All their study of the glories of theology and formal liturgy and worship for example, never prepared them for the reality of what one Baptist minister described to me as "the worship wars" in his congregation. Half of his people wanted traditional old hymns sung by a choir and the other half wanted contemporary Christian music in order to draw young people in. Neither side would give in.

So, as a spiritual director, you may know ten different ways of praying, but if you are going to operate a full-time practice, you also need a business plan, suitable location, knowledge of how to operate office equipment, liability insurance, financial record-keeping knowledge, forms, and a system of record-keeping for clients. These may be boring and tedious, but they are the necessary facts and acts of developing an effective practice. However, you will find that your Higher Power is right in the midst of all this too. You could ask your Higher Power to help you to have the strength and wisdom to persevere in faithfully doing the boring and tedious things that are necessary nuts and bolts of developing an effective practice.

The Practice Plan

I once presented my workshop on developing a full-time spiritual direction practice to a group of spiritual direction interns who had engaged in many creative practices in the course of their training. I sensed their restlessness as I hit them with practical reality after practical reality. The tension was finally broken when one of the program staff exclaimed "Oh well, I guess you can only dance your business plan for so long!" After that, the interns settled down, got serious, and ate up the rest of the workshop.

Most interns, I find, want to hear about reality. They want to know how to practically develop a spiritual direction practice after spending two years and usually three to five thousand dollars of their hard-earned money to get trained as a spiritual director. My workshop is usually greeted with relief, enthusiasm, and thankfulness towards the training coordinators for arranging to have this workshop, as it rounds out and completes the interns' training.

The field of spiritual direction is mainly populated by people who are intuitive feelers (of which I am one) rather than sensory thinkers, and therefore we don't give as much thought as we should to practical, down-to-earth realities when we are training interns.

If interns do not have some kind of practice plan, no matter how informal, they will not go anywhere. As they say in the business world, "If you fail to plan, you are planning to fail."

You need a practice plan to make your mission statement into a reality. A practice or business plan does not have to be onerous, just a general outline of how you are going to proceed. It can be as simple as writing down what you already have in your head from reading this book. You may already have in mind possible directees you want to contact and professionals with whom you want to network. So plan to jot down a list of these people and then prioritize them according to how likely it is that your contact with them will result in new clients for your practice. Then write down all your ideas about the things mentioned below: practice name, location, physical resources and human resources needed, and start to organize all of it.

Be open to constant changes in your plan. You will find that new ideas are always coming up. You will probably revamp your practice plan many times, and so you will need to balance spontaneity and planning. Do not plan things to death at the beginning so that you get paralyzed and never take action. Still, you will do much better, and work much more effectively, if you have a plan than if you don't have one.

The Practice Name

With regards to spiritual direction, if we call ourselves "Christian counselors" it may sound narrow and fundamentalist (and besides there are Jewish and Buddhist spiritual directors), and if we call ourselves "spiritual counselors," people may think we are part of the so-called New Age movement.

On the other hand, "spiritual companion" or "spiritual friend" may sound too unprofessional or too intimate to other professionals or potential clients who barely know you. It will also make it hard to charge a fee. Would you expect to pay someone who says they are your spiritual friend or companion?

Probably the only real solution is to keep the term "spiritual direction" and have every spiritual director engage in a public education campaign about what spiritual direction is and is not. We need to help people distinguish between psychological counseling (which focuses on therapy using nonreligious means), pastoral counseling (which focuses on therapy using religious means), New Age counseling (which focuses on spiritual transformation using esoteric spiritual methods) and spiritual direction (which focuses on spiritual transformation using the traditional methods of the major world religions).

Beyond what to call our field in general, it can also be important to choose a name for your practice. The possibilities are endless, but some books on developing a therapy practice recommend that, since people trust institutions more than individuals, you can increase referrals by adopting a name that suggests something bigger than just you. For example, if you were looking in the phone book for help with your marriage, who would you trust more, "The Couples Institute" or "Peter Lang"? Similarly, if you were looking for a spiritual director, would you trust "The Spiritual Direction Center" or "Ken Tobin"? (I have changed the names of the individuals to protect their identity.) Most of us would expect to receive professional counseling from the Institute or the Center, whereas we would not be so sure about the quality of the counseling from an individual if we knew nothing about them. Personally, I don't think it would be ethical to choose a name that suggests a larger organization if you are on your own, but if a group of two or more spiritual directors got together it might be worth pondering.

If you choose a practice name, try to be aware of all the subtle connotations, both positive and negative that the name might conjure up for other people. In any case, whether you choose a practice name like "SoulSearch" or "SpiritWorks," which sound very catchy and exotic and conjure up all kinds of interesting images, or some more institutional-sounding name, or whether you just call your practice by your own name, it doesn't really matter in the long run. It is not the name but the quality of service you provide, clients feeling like they are getting their spiritual needs met, and word-of-mouth, that will eventually build your practice. However, a cool name for your practice may positively change the way *you* think about what you are doing.

Location: Home Or Office Or Home-Office?

Location is not, as they say in the real estate business, "everything," but it is important. It is true that people will drive long distances to see a good spiritual counselor, and people will even travel around the world to receive a word from a "spiritual master"—a guru or rabbi who has made a name for himself through his wisdom. However, this is more the exception than the rule.

Your office, whether in or outside the home, should be central to a large enough population to support your practice. If people are going to see you face-to-face, they shouldn't have to drive too far to get there. Driving time may not concern you, because you are not the one doing the driving, but it is something clients will factor into the equation when it comes to thinking about whether spiritual counseling is worth their time, money, and effort. Location can be a determining factor in a client continuing in spiritual counseling or not. As gasoline prices rise, location becomes more important. Beyond their hour with you, and your fee, clients have to factor in travel time and gas expenses. With email, Skype, and lower long distance phoning charges, location is perhaps less important than it was, but spiritual counseling is still best done face-to-face.

Whether you work at home or outside the home, there are certain necessities you will need to have in place. First of all, your location needs to be safe for clients. It should be well-lit at night and have adequate, nearby parking spaces.

You will need a bathroom for clients because people often feel nervous about approaching a spiritual counselor, or may have come from a distance. You will need to make sure your bathroom is clean before clients arrive.

You will need a waiting room, not because you will have ten people waiting to see you, as with a doctor's office, but because people will come early to the sessions before you are ready to see them. If your home is too small to have a waiting room, you may have to ask your clients to please wait in their car until the appointed time of the session.

You can set up your waiting room to prepare people for the spiritual counseling session. Soft music can help them relax. Religious pictures or pictures of beautiful nature scenes: mountains, lakes, lotus flowers, and so on can help them get into a contemplative mood.

If you are working with interfaith clients, rather than removing all religious symbols and pictures so as not to offend anyone, include pictures and symbols from all the major traditions. In my waiting room and spiritual direction space, I have symbols, pictures, artifacts, and quotes from Judaism, Christianity, Buddhism, and Islam as well as a wonderful poster that shows that the Golden Rule is found in all religions. I also have a painting of a feminine creator of the world.

You can also put your business cards and brochures in your waiting room for clients to take and give to others. As well, you could have spiritual direction books and journals such as *Presence* in your waiting room for clients to peruse. I have a whole bookcase of CDs, DVDs and books on spirituality in my waiting room. If clients want to borrow them, they can sign them out with me and there is no charge for doing so.

One summer I visited ten psychologists and social workers in order to find reliable people to whom I could refer clients, if necessary. While sitting in their waiting rooms, I noticed four things. In almost all of them, the degrees and certificates of the practitioners were located on the waiting room wall so that you could easily read them. This reassures their clients that these practitioners have the qualifications to do a competent job.

The second thing I noticed was privacy. In two of the ten cases, while I was sitting in the waiting room, I could hear everything that was being said in the counseling session. So, I will not be referring clients to those counselors. Make sure that people sitting in your waiting room cannot overhear what is going on in your spiritual counseling sessions by having your partner or a friend sit in the waiting room while, behind closed doors and by yourself, you talk fairly loudly in your counseling space. You may have to put padding around your office door to make it soundproof.

The third thing I noticed was the furnishings, whether they were comfortable or not. Beyond a sense of physical comfort, clients will get a sense of whether your practice is thriving or not by your furnishings in your waiting room and spiritual counseling space. If things look dilapidated and run down, or well-appointed and well taken care of, clients will notice.

One therapist did not actually have a waiting room, just a chair in a hallway of her home. There were no signs indicating which rooms were the bathroom or her office, the wallpaper in her office was peeling and torn, and the slats on the horizontal blinds were bent out of place. Although she was a nice person, her furnishings made me wonder about her professionalism.

A friend told me that he didn't go back for a second session with a spiritual director because, although she was known as a "crone," that is, a "wise woman," her house smelled of old dog, and the first thing he noticed, before he even got inside, was that her threshold had not been swept in what looked like years. Also there was too much traffic noise from a busy avenue outside the counseling room that made it difficult for him to relax and open up. Her home was not conducive to her work, and all of this added up to "definitely not presenting a good image" he said.

The fourth thing I noticed was whether their offices were in an office building or their home. Some psychologists, social workers, and spiritual directors feel that they are not really professionals, and therefore cannot take their practice seriously, unless they have an office separate from their home.

Having a home office is a popular alternative, and has a number of advantages and disadvantages when compared to working out of an office building. One of the biggest advantages of a home office is that, first of all, there is no rent to pay, and secondly, you can write-off (take off your income to lower the income tax you pay) so many things. (Home expense write-offs will be covered in depth in a later chapter.) Having a home office means as well that you save a lot of money and time that you would spend driving to and from work.

The main disadvantages of a home office are that, first of all, it may not seem as professional to your clients. Secondly, it can be too easy for you to get distracted by other people in your home (notably your spouse and children, if you have them), or by cleaning or recreational activities around the house (magazines, television, the Internet, etc.) Also, you don't have the advantage of work and home separation—it can feel like you are always on the job. Finally, you may suffer from a sense of isolation from colleagues and the rest of the world.

On the other hand, you can fix up your home office so it looks professional. Distractions can be handled with a bit of self-discipline. You can separate work and family life by confining your work to one area of the house. As well, you can overcome isolation by having lunch with colleagues or friends, by getting into a peer supervision group, getting involved with a church or other organization such as a service club, facilitating workshops and retreats, and so on.

The big advantage of having an office in an office building is that it can give you a more central location than your home, as well as a sense of professionalism and credibility with your clients. The downside is the cost of renting and maintaining an office.

One solution to this, as was mentioned earlier, would be to band together with other spiritual counselors, alternative health practitioners, and therapists, and start your own center. That way you would be co-renting with five to ten others. Another alternative, if you can afford it, would be to buy a building and sublet offices in it to others. Then, of course, you will have to worry about overall maintenance, parking spaces, financial issues, building security, and janitorial staff. You could charge the other tenants enough rent to cover all this, but you may not want to become a building administrator, although, then again, perhaps this could be your part-time work while you build your spiritual direction practice.

The higher your costs as a spiritual counselor, the more you have to pass on your costs to your clients by charging higher fees, which may result in fewer clients and higher turnover. So the best solution for most spiritual counselors will be to work out of their home.

Physical Resources

Any large business supply store will have all you need in terms of office supplies, office furniture, and business equipment. Besides a good computer, I would recommend buying a photocopier. They are inexpensive to buy and invaluable to own. I use mine regularly for copying relevant handouts which I give to the client when the session is over, which helps the client to get more out of the spiritual direction sessions, which ensures client loyalty, which keeps my practice going, which pays for my expenses like copiers and other overhead expenses.

Large business supply stores may also offer the services of graphic artists to help you with the creation of customized logos, business cards, and brochures. As well, you will usually be able to do inexpensive photocopying at the store if you don't buy your own copier, and pick up books on computers and how to do financial record-keeping. They may also make signs for office doors or you may have to go to a store that specializes in making signs. Check your local Yellow Pages.

Human Resources

This book can be like a good business coach to you, but if you want a live coach, you could search the Internet for local business coaches and then interview three or four to see whom you feel most comfortable with. It would be important to work with someone who is sensitive to spiritual issues.

If you think you need them, you could find good lawyers, financial planners, and retirement experts through inquiring with local psychology or social work associations. Or, you might be able to get inexpensive or even free help on legal, public relations, marketing, and accounting issues from students at local colleges or universities. University, college, or public librarians could help you with audio-visual aids. You may be able to get help with all this for free in online discussion groups.

You could hire an accountant to keep your financial records in order and do your income tax, or you could do your own financial record-keeping and hire an income tax specialist. Financial record-keeping is not hard. All you have to do is buy a record-keeping book from a business supply store, divide it into categories like "office expenses," "car and travel," "advertising," "education," and "home expenses," keep your receipts every time you make a purchase, and then from your receipts record all your expenditures in these areas once a month.

You should have a notebook in your car to record every practice-related trip: date, destination, and mileage. Be sure to keep all your receipts for every practice item you spend money on in labeled file folders in case you get audited for income tax purposes. You will also need to keep ongoing records of all your income from directees, workshops, and other sources.

Here are some of the things you can write-off in most countries, provinces, and states (consult with local experts what specifically applies in your area). These are expenses you can deduct from your income to substantially lower your income taxes (pay particular attention to car and home expenses):

Small Business Write-Offs

- accounting/income tax preparation fees
- advertising
- bad debts (people not paying you)
- spiritual direction/supervision/counseling fees (fees your spiritual director, supervisor, or therapist has charged you)
- car expenses: divide your business miles by the total of your personal and business miles to get the percentage of your car expenses you can write off. You can then claim that percentage of the following car expenses: license and registration fees/gas/oil/insurance/interest on car loans or leasing fees/car depreciation/maintenance and repairs/miscellaneous car expenses: car wash, tires, parking, etc.
- capital costs: cost of business equipment, furniture, etc.
- facilitation expenses (markers, masking tape, etc.)
- pension plan contributions
- education costs: tuition for workshops, courses, conferences, retreats, books, DVDs and CDs, periodicals (could also include the expense of lost/unreturned books, DVDs and CDs, although this could also come under bad debts or program expenses)
- home expenses: calculate what percentage of your house your practice takes up (including your office, washroom, hallways, waiting room, etc.) You can then claim that percentage of the following home expenses: fire insurance/gas (heat)/hydro (electricity/water)/mortgage interest/property taxes/repairs and maintenance
- the percentage of telephone expenses (including service fees and long distance) used for business
- membership fees
- miscellaneous business expenses (office cleaning, distilled water, paper cups, etc.)
- office expenses: xeroxing, postage, cartridges (printers, fax, etc), office supplies (paper, pads, pens, envelopes, folders, etc.)

- program expenses: markers, tape, DVDs, CDs, and books for clients

- travel: rental car expenses/plane/meals and entertainment/ accommodations (hotels, etc.)

Insurance and Incorporation

As mentioned earlier, all spiritual directors need to be in a constant process of educating the public about spiritual direction. People need to know that it is meant to support spiritual growth, that it is not therapy, and Spiritual Directors International is an educational organization and not an accrediting or credentialing association.

This is important because in North America we live in a "litigious" society, that is, as a spiritual director you may be sued by one of your clients, and you need to know about steps you can take to protect yourself.

First of all, you need to educate the public and your clients that you are not there to give advice, but just to explore possible ways of growing spiritually and the possible consequences of certain actions a client may be contemplating. All *decisions* are left in the hands of the client.

If you gave financial advice, for example, "Sell all you have and give it to the poor," this may have worked in biblical times, but nowadays you could be sued by your client's relatives. The other main thing you could be sued for is stepping over a client's sexual boundaries. The problem here is the interpretation of what is appropriate. You might think it is appropriate to give your clients a hug at the end of the session, but one of them may think it transgresses their boundaries, particularly if they have a history of sexual abuse. Personally, I never hug my clients unless they initiate it.

The best thing you or any spiritual counselor can do is to follow the "Guidelines for Ethical Conduct in Spiritual Direction" worked out by Spiritual Directors International. Copies can be ordered from www.sdiworld.org.

Beyond that, all spiritual directors should have liability insurance. Getting this insurance can be challenging because most insurance companies will not know what spiritual direction is, and even if they did, they may not cover you because there is no overarching professional body that certifies or licenses you. Here in Canada, through an insurance broker who works with a lot of different insurance companies, I have worked out a policy that covers me as an individual in private practice.

If you can get into a group plan the fees will be a lot lower because they are insuring vast numbers of people. In the United States, the American Professional Agency and the American Association of Christian Counselors will insure spiritual directors relatively cheaply (a few hundred dollars a year) for professional and premises liability (malpractice and accidents or injury). There are probably similar associations in most countries. If you are a member of SDI, you can get more information about liability in the "Members Only" section of the web site of Spiritual Directors International at www.sdiworld.org.

After consulting several lawyers, Spiritual Directors International developed a list of things you can do to reduce liability risk.   First of all, know your own limitations. If a person needs social work, psychological, medical, or financial support, make appropriate referrals to service providers you know and trust. Secondly, you could use an Engagement Agreement which clearly states you are not a mental health professional or therapist, and which also spells out the nature of a healthy spiritual direction relationship. You and the client both date and sign the agreement and keep a copy. Thirdly, give each client a copy of the "Guidelines for Ethical Conduct in Spiritual Direction."

Here is a sample consent form:

Spiritual Direction Consent Form
    I_____, hereby consent to: participate in spiritual direction with _____
(include credentials), and the agreed upon fee will be $_____ per session, payable as fee for service or as negotiated; and understanding that _____ (director) is a member of Spiritual Directors International, which has an established code of ethics under which she/he practices;

I also understand that she/he is currently under supervision for her/his work so that she/he can better respond to my needs; and while our sessions together are not counseling or therapy, healing may occur during our sessions together.

Signature of Client:_____

Date: _____

Signature of Director:_____

Date:_____

Another avenue to consider to protect yourself is to incorporate, so that your practice is considered a corporation. This is costly, but you only need to do it once rather than yearly. You are then liable only for what belongs to the corporation (for example, computers, bookcases, etc.) They cannot sue you for your big assets such as your house or car.

The problem with incorporation, according to my own lawyer, is that your client must know at all times that they are dealing with a corporation not an individual, or you are still liable to be personally sued. So on your letterhead, signs, brochures, and business cards, you have to include "inc." after your practice name or your personal name.

Another option recommended by my lawyer is to simply put your major assets in your spouse's or parents' name if and when you think someone is going to sue you. This can be done quickly and cheaply and might be the best option if you think North American spiritual directors are being too paranoid about being sued. I have talked to several Canadian psychologists who have been in full-time private practice for twenty years or more and who said no one had ever tried to sue them. There is probably less chance of being sued as a spiritual director than as a psychologist, but every spiritual director needs to make their own decision about this, and it is better to be safe than sorry.

Forms

Some trainers of spiritual directors who have never had their own practice, or who have just seen a few people a week for spiritual direction, have balked when I suggested that, to run a full-time practice properly, you need forms. Creating forms is an inevitable part of developing a full-time spiritual counseling practice. You might be able to work without forms if you just have a few clients, but when you reach a certain size, forms become necessary.

It helps, for example, to have a basic intake form where you record all your client's contact information, marital and employment status, reasons for coming to spiritual counseling, Myers Briggs and Enneagram scores and so on. Here is a sample "Intake Form."

Intake Form

Date:_____ How Heard About Me?_____

Referral Thanked?_____

Name:_____

Call the night before?_____

Address:_____Zip/Postal Code:_____

Home Phone:_____Work Phone:_____

Cell/Pager:_____ Email:_____

Marital Status:_____ Spouse's Name:_____

Children's Names and Ages:_____

Employment Status: (U/FT/PT/STUDENT/RETIRED)_____

Type of Work:_____

Church or Spiritual Organization:_____

Priest/Minister/Pastor:_____

Church or Spiritual Activities/Groups:_____

Myers Briggs Type (and scores):_____

Enneagram Type (and scores):_____

Reason for Coming to Spiritual Direction: _____

_____

Contacts:_____

_____

Notes:_____

_____

_____

At the end of the first session, I give my clients a handout that outlines my office policies. This tells my clients what to expect from spiritual direction and what I expect from them. It also tells them how to get the most out of spiritual direction. As well, it contains my qualifications, a list of services I provide, as well as policies around appointments, referrals, fees, and termination of sessions. Here is a sample "Office Policies Form." The title which my clients see is "Spiritual Direction: Helpful Information."

Spiritual Direction: Helpful Information

Welcome to Spiritual Direction

Spiritual direction is many faceted and can include:

- guidance for growth in your image of God and in methods of prayer
- help in finding God (however you conceive God to be) in life's challenges
- assistance in discerning God's will
- help with inner healing work and dream work
- companionship for the spiritual journey

During a typical spiritual direction session the directee (person taking spiritual direction) might share about relationships, family, choices, loss, goals, work, illness, or various struggles. The spiritual director's primary task is to help you notice God's action in all this and how you are responding to these divine initiatives.

Spiritual direction has some similarities to therapy, yet is different from it. Like good therapy it is client-centered and non-directive, that is, the director tries to draw out of you what you need to do rather than giving advice. However, spiritual direction is about your relationship with the Divine, not about emotional therapy, and the ultimate spiritual director is believed to be God. The human spiritual director is a trained guide who can help you in your relationship with the Divine.

Emotional relief is often a valued byproduct, but spiritual direction is different from therapy. Spiritual direction looks at your total spiritual formation, which can bring greater purpose and meaning to your life.

How Can I Benefit the Most?

To enhance the spiritual direction process, directees prepare for sessions by thinking about several things they want to discuss (see sample preparation questions below). They also take notes during or after the session on key points, review their notes several times before the next session, and follow up on things the spiritual director recommends.

Directees who gain the most also understand that spiritual growth takes time, effort, and patience and that, although some sessions may not feel fruitful on the surface, there may be subtle shifts occurring subconsciously.

Spiritual Direction Preparation Questions

The questions below can help you prepare for your spiritual direction session:

1. Where am I now in my life—my personal life, my professional life, my creative life, my believing life? Am I where I want to be in all of these areas of my life? How did I get to this place in my life?

2. What are my questions, doubts, confusions?

3. How has my spiritual life been in the past few months? Rich, full, boring, chaotic?

4. What events, experiences, relationships, etc. have given me a sense of God's presence or absence?

5. How do I feel about my relationship with God, and about God's relationship with me right now?

6. Which life decisions have me wondering what God's will is for me?

7. In what area(s) of my life do I sense God calling me to grow or to let go of something?

8. How have I been connecting with God, my soul, or the universe in the past few months (prayer, meditation, music, walking in the woods, etc)? How often, and how satisfying have each of these been? Is the experience as fulfilling as I'd like?

9. How can my spiritual director help me address the empty or uncertain areas of my life, so that I can feel vibrant, whole, and connected once more?

10. Is there anything else I would like to talk about with my spiritual director?

Additional Services

Beyond regular spiritual direction you might want to take advantage of the following services:

- Programs that can be worked on at home and then explored within a spiritual direction context:

Experiencing the Heart of Jesus (workbook by Max Lucado)
The Cup of Our Life (workbook by Joyce Rupp)
The Purpose Driven Life (40 day program by Rick Warren)
Scripture Study (using daily readings)

- Spiritual direction using the Myers Briggs Personality Inventory or the Enneagram

- Talks, workshops, and retreats on all kinds of spiritual topics by Bruce

- Free borrowing of books, CDs, DVDs

- Free helpful spirituality articles emailed to all directees approximately every month

- Grief counseling

- Marriage coaching and marriage preparation courses

The Spiritual Director

I graduated with distinction in May 2003 with a Doctor of Ministry degree in Spiritual Direction from the Graduate Theological Foundation which is affiliated with Oxford University in England. I am the past director of two adult religious education centres in London and Sarnia.

I am a member of Spiritual Directors International and Spiritual Directors of Ontario and adhere to their standards of professional ethics regarding confidentiality, boundaries, and privacy.

I have given workshops and retreats across Canada and the United States. I've published many articles in both religious and secular journals. My book *Archetypes for Spiritual Direction: Discovering the Heroes Within* was published by Paulist Press in September 2005.

I welcome people of all beliefs and I am committed to reverence for the dignity, equality, rights, and gifts of all persons. I welcome and accept everyone wherever they are spiritually.

Appointments

The appointment time has been reserved for you. Forty-eight hours notice is required for appointment changes or cancellation so that the time may be given to someone else.

I realize there are last minute circumstances such as inclement weather, illness, or accidents where you need to cancel or reschedule within the 48 hour limit, but if the circumstances are not exceptional, you will be required to pay for the session.

Also please call ahead if you will be late for an appointment. Depending on my schedule, you may still be able to do the full hour, or the time may be limited to the remaining portion of the originally scheduled hour.

Sessions usually last for 1 hour and wrap up at 5 minutes to the hour to allow time for a closing prayer and to schedule another session.

Spiritual Direction Hours

Monday: 6:00 to 9:00pm
Tues, Wedn, Thurs: 1:30 to 9:00pm
Friday and Saturday: 9am to 4:30pm
These hours can be adjusted somewhat to meet your needs.

How Often Do We Meet?

This will be determined by a mutual decision at our first meeting. Depending on your individual needs we can meet as often as once a week or as seldom as once every few months. For sustained growth and progress though, it is recommended that you meet with your spiritual director at least once a month.

Spiritual direction can take place for just a few sessions or for many years. Most monthly directees maintain their sessions for at least a year. Others see the value of regular, ongoing feedback throughout their spiritual life.

Referrals to Others

After discussion and with your consent, I may recommend that you see other counselors such as psychologists or social workers if I think it would be helpful. This does not mean you need to stop spiritual direction with me.

Referrals to Dr. Tallman

You can refer your family members, relatives, friends, and co-workers. All are welcome.

Fees and Payment

In order to accommodate different income levels, fees are $50 to $90. (The Harmonized Sales Tax is included, not additional). Directees pay whatever they decide is financially sustainable for them within this range. My hope is that well-off directees will pay at the top end of the scale so that less well-off directees can pay at the lower end of the scale. In cases of financial difficulty, arrangements can be made to suit your situation. Financial hardship should not be a barrier to experiencing spiritual direction.

Payment by cash or cheque is fine. Please do not post-date cheques and please pay at the start of the session. It can be uncomfortable to have to remind people to pay just as they are walking out the door.

Special Circumstances

Spiritual direction is best done in person. However, to accommodate special circumstances, such as snow or distance, spiritual direction can be done by telephone or online (Skype). For distance sessions payment at the above rates is mailed to me. There are no long-distance phone charges.

Reviews and Termination of Sessions

Periodic reviews of your spiritual direction sessions can be helpful to raise your awareness of your progress. You will fill out a Spiritual Direction Review form which looks at your progress and what you want to work on next.

I support healthy termination of sessions. If you are planning to terminate spiritual direction, it works best if you let me know at least twenty-four hours before your last session. The final wrap-up session gives us the opportunity to talk about our time together, tie up any loose ends, get closure, and part in a positive way.

Questions or Concerns

Please do not hesitate to ask if you have questions or concerns. I am here to help and serve you.

I pray for each directee on a regular basis, and ask that you similarly pray for me. With prayer God does great things through us, changing our lives and the world around us.

Peace and blessings,
Dr. Bruce Tallman

It is also helpful to have a form on which to record the results of the periodic reviews you do of the spiritual counseling sessions. As mentioned earlier, regular reviews can be an opportunity to note the client's progress, which can be important in keeping clients motivated. It is important to specify up front that your intention is not to terminate the sessions but simply to note progress. It is a good idea to periodically review where we have come from and where we want to go. However, if you do want to terminate the sessions, you can use this form for that as well. Go through this form with your client whenever you deem it appropriate. Here is a sample "Spiritual Direction Review Form":

Spiritual Direction Review Form

1. A. What was your original goal in coming to spiritual direction? B. Was that goal achieved?

2. A. If that goal was achieved—how?
    B. If not, how could it be achieved?

3. What benefitted you the most from these spiritual direction sessions?

4. What benefitted you the least or hindered your growth?

5. A. What changes, if any, did you notice in yourself? What were the changes in your prayer life, spirituality or your life in general?
   B. How did these changes happen?

6. A. What did you learn about yourself or what new understandings did you have?
   B. Any surprises?

7. What did the spiritual director do well? (For example, welcoming/hospitality, praying, questioning, listening, sympathizing, discerning, supporting, affirming or anything else?) Was there anything he did that particularly helped you?

8. What areas does the spiritual director need to work on? Was there anything that bothered, blocked, or hindered you in any way?

9. What areas do you think you need to grow in? What would you like to work on in the future?

10. If there was one thing you could change about the way things were done, what would that be?

11. Any comments on the spacing and length of sessions? The setting/location? comfort? privacy? confidentiality?

12. Any other thoughts, feelings, insights, comments about anything?

13. Director's assessment of client's growth. (This is a chance for positive encouragement.)

Business Cards

You can make simple yet professional looking business cards on your computer and print them on special business card stock you can buy at any paper supplies store. Most word-processing programs like Corel Wordperfect or Microsoft Word have templates for making business cards. (For example, in Wordperfect 8.0 you simply bring up a Wordperfect document on your computer screen, click on "New", and scroll down to "Business Card" and click on it and then design your own card.) Business card stock is perforated so there is no cutting involved on your part. Business cards can also be professionally designed and printed, although this can be expensive, about three times the cost of making your own. At the start, it's probably best to do them yourself and then see if you hand them out enough, and get enough results back to justify paying for professional design. On the other hand, you are more likely to hand them out if they are really attractively designed by a professional.

Letterhead

You can also easily make your own letterhead on your computer. For spiritual directors, a good way to increase your credibility, particularly with professionals, is to join Spiritual Directors International and put on the bottom of your letterhead "Member, Spiritual Directors International." Professionals will take note that you belong to a larger organizational body and are not just operating on your own with some weird new thing called "spiritual direction" (which many professionals will never have heard of). If you have a web site, include that on your letterhead as well so that professionals and non-professionals can further check you out.

Receipts

At some point, some of your clients may ask you for a receipt for all the money they paid you. You can make up standard receipt or invoice forms on your computer or buy them at your local business supply store. If spiritual counseling can be considered as a business expense or income tax write-off for your clients, it could save them from fifteen to fifty percent of your fee. So be sure to ask them, particularly if they are self-employed, if spiritual counseling is something they can claim for business or income tax purposes, and let them know you will be glad to give them receipts.

CHAPTER SEVENTEEN

Fees

Discussing money is always difficult, especially for spiritually-oriented people such as spiritual counselors. Therefore, I hope that this chapter does not offend some of my readers. We do live in the real world, where money is very important. The following are some facts of life which I have discovered from living in reality as a full-time spiritual director since 2002.

Mindset

Being a full-time spiritual counselor requires being mature about money and learning how to control and manage it so that you are in control of your finances rather than your finances controlling you. You want to make enough money so that you don't have to worry about money all the time.

You have to have a mature mindset when it comes to reconciling your service and your fee. The bottom-line mindset as a spiritual director is to always trust that if you put service and ethics first, everything else will follow.

When it comes to charging a fee for your services as a spiritual counselor, it is important to remember several things based on the world we live in.

First of all, whether you call what you do "charging a fee" or "asking for a donation," both will be open to legal liability if someone decides to sue you. Lawyers would argue that it is just a matter of semantics.

Secondly, remember that *people have money*, and paying for your services is the client's issue, not yours. Don't think that clients will not pay if you charge a fee that is really a just and fair amount for your services. Low fees will not necessarily mean more clients. Lower fees may just mean that people will disrespect your services. They will take the attitude that if it doesn't cost very much, it cannot be worth very much. People are used to paying a professional fee for services for their car, teeth, and bodies. The big question is: do people *want* your services? If they do, they will pay, within certain reasonable limits. If they don't want your services, it doesn't matter how low your fees are. You could offer spiritual counseling for free, and they still wouldn't come.

If you are a spiritual director, remember that no one does spiritual direction for free. Everyone gets paid either directly or indirectly. One woman said she couldn't believe I was charging for spiritual direction because she could go to her priest and get it for free. I reminded her that her priest was not offering it for free. He was paid a salary for doing spiritual direction and other things as well. The same applies to all ministers and people in religious orders.

The next thing you need to remember is that the value of money is very nebulous and very relative to many factors. When I started doing spiritual direction full-time, my fee scale was $20 to $40 because that seemed to be the going rate for spiritual direction in my city. When after about a year, I woke up to the fact that it was mainly nuns doing spiritual direction, and that I was not a nun, I decided that, as a married man with children, I needed to raise my fee scale. So I gradually raised it to where it is now, that is, $50 to $90. Now when a person pays me $50 at the low end of my scale, they think they are getting a bargain, even though they are paying more than the high end of my previous scale. I don't rejoice in this, and don't think I am ripping anyone off, I am just charging what I need to in order to make a modest living at this.

Money is a very psychological thing. My wife Grace and I recently decided to sell a fridge and stove we never used in order to make more room in our home. We just wanted to get rid of them, so we advertised them for $100 ($50 each.) A woman offered us $80 for the two of them. If we had advertised them for $200, she would probably have offered us $160, and felt very satisfied with herself if we accepted her offer, even though she was paying double what she would have in the first instance. We once had a garage sale, and were selling perfectly good CDs for $1 that we had paid $20 for, simply because we no longer listened to them and wanted to make room on our CD rack for newer musicians. One man offered us twenty cents per CD. People have a psychological, ego need to feel they are getting something at a special rate, even though it is all very relative and arbitrary.

It is extremely difficult to evaluate the value of a service. In London, Ontario where I live, dental hygienists (after a year's training in a community college) charge $48 per cleaning, which usually takes about twenty minutes. They are working with peoples' teeth. I am working with peoples' immortal souls. Which is more important? Most social workers and psychologists in private practice in my city are charging $90 to $150 per hour. They are dealing with peoples' behavior and emotional well-being while they are on Earth. I am potentially dealing with peoples' eternal destinies. Are their services really almost twice as valuable as mine? How does one evaluate the dollar value of anything as nebulous as spiritual growth?

How much your services are worth to a person will be relative to such things as how much money they have, how tight they are with money, their priorities in life, their personality type, whether they are married with children or single, and so on. For example, when you state that your fee is $60 an hour, a person might go through the following mental machinations:

- this is cheaper than what psychologists are charging
- I could easily spend $600 getting my car repaired
- I want to make spirituality a priority in my life
- if I make spirituality a priority in my life I will feel better and get along with my spouse and children better. How much is that worth?

- it is only once a month
- what's the meaning of life anyway? Is it just an endless rat race? I need to find some meaning
- they say that people who meditate and pray live longer
- my spouse thinks nothing of going to a therapist. I need to take care of myself too.
- etc.

So, the dollar amount of your fee is only one factor people will take into consideration when trying to figure out if they want to give spiritual counseling a try or not.

We are in spiritual counseling because we want to help people grow spiritually not because we want to get rich. Charge enough so that you can survive. The goal is ongoing survival so that you can continue to help people spiritually.

As a spiritual counselor, you want to establish a fair, flexible, and professional fee that causes no financial hardship to your clients or to you. In order to be fair to yourself, you may have to raise your fee.

On the one hand, higher fees may mean less word-of-mouth advertising, fewer referrals, fewer clients, and more dropouts. On the other hand, your fee can make you look like an expert or not. Higher fees may mean that people will think you must be a great spiritual counselor if you charge that much; your clients might take spiritual counseling more seriously since they are paying so much for it; they may put more into it to get their money's worth, and therefore they may get more out of it, stick with it longer, tell more people about it, and you may end up with more referrals and more clients. Raising your fee might actually attract more clients.

In our market-centered world, customers become suspicious when something sells for much less than similar products. A friend of mine was in charge of a supermarket. They accidentally over-ordered a shipment of eggs, and so they reduced the prices in an attempt to get rid of their excess stock. Nobody bought them. So they doubled the price compared to similar eggs and people snapped them up!

Charging a higher fee might allow you to pay for more profes-sional-looking brochures, a more attractive web site, more comfortable office furniture so your clients feel more relaxed, and a safer, more central location for your clients. Higher fees may allow you to buy up-to-date books, CD's and DVD's that your clients can borrow and benefit from. Higher fees may also mean that you can go to more conferences and workshops, and have more time to study, so that you constantly become a better spiritual counselor. In short, higher fees may allow you to serve and care for your clients much better. They will be paying a higher rate, but getting better service. Most people do not mind this. What they *do* object to is paying a high fee for poor service.

When you are discussing your fee, there is no need to be shy or timid. In fact, a faltering voice or an air of uncertainty on your part will convey to the client that you do not feel right charging this much. Uncertainty on your part will cause suspicion on their part. Fees should be discussed openly and candidly in a self-assured, forthright, and matter-of-fact manner.

Money Shadow

Some spiritual counselors may fail because of their negative mind set about money, their "money shadow." They may equate money with materialism, the opposite of spirituality. They may believe money is a vile thing or something they can totally disregard. I've been there and done that.

Or they may have a scarcity consciousness, believing that money is in short supply.

They may remember Jesus saying that it's easier for a camel to pass through the eye of a needle than for a rich person to get into heaven, or Jesus blasting the unjust rich, or clearing the temple of moneychangers.

All this is very scriptural, but it is not money that is the problem. The problem is the *love* of money. Jesus was addressing people who put money ahead of people, and therefore made money into their god and treated people unfairly.

Money itself is morally neutral. It is what is in our hearts that causes us to give alms or hoard money and act unjustly. Money can be used for positive purposes such as buying a better copier so you can more readily give clients take-home handouts to meditate on, and other positive purposes such as those mentioned under "mind-set" above. It is not money but what we do with it, what we use it for, that is good or evil.

On the other hand, other spiritual directors may fail because they make money into an idol. They believe money is everything, and work so hard to get it that they burn themselves out and end up quitting their practice. If they see clients as dollar signs and put profits before people they will kill the spirit and soul of spiritual direction. They will inevitably do things in subtly manipulative ways that people will see through. This is an effective way to destroy word-of-mouth promotion and drive people away.

Spiritual counselors may also have no idea how to balance their practice so that they go through "boom periods" when everything is flowing well, and "bust periods" when things slow down. The result is that they feel alternately high or depressed. It is during the low points that people are tempted to quit. Or, because of their money shadow, spiritual counselors may fear that if they confront a difficult or aggressive client, the client will leave. Or they may be afraid to raise their fees for the same reason.

The money shadow can cause us to set our fees based on many false notions. Fees should not be set on the basis of your fears about keeping or losing clients, your lack of self-worth, or your guilt or confusion about how to integrate fees and service. Fees should be set on the basis of logic and fairness to yourself and your clients. What is a fair price based on your services, your years of training and experience, your vision for your practice, and your plans for the future?

When clients pay you for a one hour session, they are not paying you for an ecstatic mystical experience, they are paying you for your time and your life-energy. Each of us has only so many units of life-energy. Money is simply something given in exchange for your life-energy. How precious is your life-energy to you? How much would you sell that hour of your life-energy for, knowing that you are never going to get it back?

Clients are also paying you for your training and your skills more than for your love. They are paying you because you are a trained spiritual counselor. Anyone can love them, but not everyone has years of training and spiritual direction or counseling skills. Naturally, you also want to love your clients, but that is not what they are paying you for.

Three Fee Options

There are three basic options regarding your fee. First of all, you could have a sliding scale based on the person's or family's gross or net income. The problem with this is that you have to find out what the person earns, and this can be a very touchy subject. Even if you have a sheet you hand your client that has a variable fee pegged to the client's income in terms of tens of thousands of dollars, when the client chooses a fee he or she is automatically telling you his or her income is in a certain range, and people are reticent to disclose this.

You also have no idea if they are being honest, and you can have situations where a woman's husband is earning $100,000 per year but he gives her none of it, or only a small allowance. She may be personally poor even while living in a wealthy family.

Another option is to have a fee range that is not directly pegged to income, and just ask the client to decide what they will pay within that range. For example, you might say "In order to try to accommodate people with different income levels, I have a fee range of $40 to $70 per hour. I trust that my wealthier clients will pay towards the top of the range so that my poorer clients can pay at the lower level and still come. Therefore I leave it up to you to decide what you can afford to pay within my range in good conscience, that is, being fair to both yourself and myself."

With both a sliding scale or a fee range, you are taking the risk of being taken advantage of. Fortunately, it usually becomes fairly obvious if someone is abusing your system, and so you can confront them about it. I was once doing spiritual direction for free with a woman because she said she could not afford to pay anything. However, after several sessions she let it slip that she took two trips a year to Italy. I confronted her with the fact that, if she could afford these trips, she could afford to pay me. She promptly paid me for all the previous sessions.

A third fee option is to have a set fee. Many spiritual directors, like me, avoid this option because they don't want to exclude poorer clients. However, it is possible to get around this by offering those who can't pay the full fee several different possibilities.

You could pro-rate the hour. In other words, if the full fee was $40 per hour, you could ask the client to pay $35 for 50 minutes, $30 for 40 minutes, or $25 for 30 minutes. Some problems with this approach are that things you do outside the session can take just as long for a half hour session as for a full hour (preparing the spiritual counseling room, washroom, and waiting room, reading your notes from the last session, praying, taking notes after), it is hard to keep a session to the exact time agreed upon, it requires a lot of clock-watching, and neither you nor the client may feel complete if the time flies by. Further, if the client has a long drive to and from the session, it may not be worthwhile for a reduced hour.

Another possibility is to have a set fee that is reduced for time slots that are harder to fill. For example, if evening is prime time, you would charge your full fee of $60. For mornings you would charge $50, and for afternoons $40.

Still another "set fee" possibility is to offer a lower rate for pre-paid "package deals." This is what piano and violin teachers do: you pay for a set number of sessions in advance. In spiritual direction the client could pay $400 in advance for ten sessions rather than paying your set fee of $60 per session. This is a $200 saving for your client and you are compensated by knowing that they will definitely be coming. This lower rate could particularly apply to a directee who wants to come each week.

Another set fee option is to invite those who cannot pay the full fee to be in a small group. Two people in a group might pay $40 each instead of the regular $60 per session. Groups can be a lot of fun, and you earn $80 per hour instead of $60. On the other hand, it can be harder to achieve the same depth with clients as in a one-to-one session, and it can take a lot more preparation to properly run a group. Also, collecting payment can be harder. You need to have a prepared agenda so that people don't just show up and chat. Otherwise, they may be less willing to pay. As well, if there are six clients, they will be justifiably perturbed if you are earning $240 per hour and not actively leading the group, or if you let one person dominate the hour.

Another flexible possibility would be to let clients come as often as *they* want instead of once per month. The idea of directees coming once a month is an unquestioned tradition in the field of spiritual direction. However, does this need to be "the way we've always done it?"

A young woman always cut off the end of the roast before she put it in the oven. When her husband pointed out that she was wasting valuable meat and asked why she did it, she said "because that's the way my mother always did it." When they asked her mother why she did it she said " because that's the way my mother always did it." When they asked the young woman's grandmother why she did it, she said "because my pan was too small."

My point is that there is often no good reason for doing things, it's just a tradition that no one questions. A priest once told me that the people in the procession at the beginning of Mass always stopped at a certain point and genuflected toward an empty corner of the church, even though the magnificent statue of Moses that used to be there had been removed years ago.

A friend of mine and I decided to go out to a movie. He must have been lost in thought as he walked up the aisle of the theater, because he absentmindedly genuflected and made the sign of the cross when he came to the row he wanted to sit in.

Sometimes we do things out of habit without thinking. As far as I know, no one has done any research on the benefits of coming once a month for spiritual direction versus the benefits of coming once a week or once every two months. It would make an interesting research project, although I am not sure how you would measure the spiritual change in the lives of the participants.

Since coming once a month is just an unquestioned tradition, why not let the client decide how often he or she wants to come? Most of my clients come once a month, but some want to come every week because they are in a spiritual crisis, and some only want to see me every three months because they feel they are making good progress on their own but they see the value in getting some objective feedback from an outside source once in a while. Some of my clients start off by coming once a week or once every two weeks and then thin it out to once a month. Some pay me $20 every three months and some pay me $85 every week.

If you wanted to switch from a sliding scale or fee range to a set amount, you could draw up a letter stating your set fee and all the possible payment options listed above. You could mail this to your clients and then discuss it with them the next time you met. You and they might want to negotiate a new fee arrangement based on these options.

You might announce to all your clients in October that the new fee system will start in February. Or you might let your present clients continue paying at their present rate, and just announce the new fee system to new clients. Or, you might only announce it to those of your present clients who are paying less than the new set fee.

Having an across-the-board set fee has the advantage of making it easier to calculate your income for a week. You just multiply your set fee times the number of sessions you have booked.

And it may seem more professional to clients. When you go to a lawyer or dentist or mechanic they usually don't have a sliding scale or a fee range based on income. "Well, you can pay between $100 and $300 to get that wisdom tooth pulled (or carburetor fixed). How much are you making anyway?" How many of us would like to hear that from a professional? Wouldn't we wonder how much the service they are providing is *really* worth and how much it cost *them* to perform this service? And how many of us like to disclose our income? On the other hand, if you say you have a fee range to accommodate people with lower incomes, in my experience most people coming to spiritual direction will understand and support that.

How To Set Fees

When setting fees there are many things you should consider such as:

- what kind of lifestyle do I want?
- what is my total practice plan?
- why do I want to earn a certain amount?
- do I need a new office, office equipment, office furniture?

- do I want to work with more or fewer clients?
- whom do I want to serve? Students? Executives? Seniors with fixed incomes?
- how fast do I want to fill my practice?
- what is the value put on spiritual direction in the community I am serving?
- what are people willing to pay?
- what are others charging?

One way to set fees is to set a preliminary fee and keep track of all your practice-related expenses for a year. Then you can estimate whether you need to raise (or lower) your fee in order to have the kind of net income you want.

Psychiatrists, consulting therapists, and executive coaches might charge $150 to $300 per hour. Psychologists, social workers, and other registered or licensed counselors might charge $75 to $150 per hour. Alternative healers such as acupuncturists, massage therapists, and energy therapists might charge $45 to $95 per hour. Spiritual directors would probably fit into this last category.

You will need to figure out which groups to target in order to get clients who will be able to pay in your fee range. It's a good idea to spend some time figuring out who your ideal client would be. For example, it might be a spiritually-oriented, professional, single, middle-aged female, or a recently divorced male. You can then think about where you would find this type of client.

Fee Calculation Guidelines

It's important to understand, first of all, that as a spiritual counselor you don't bill your clients for every expense you incur (such as office supplies). You only bill your clients for contact time, not administrative time. Therefore, your contact fee must include both your contact time and your unbilled services, in other words, your total expenses.

Fee Calculation Based On Gross Income

$50,000 gross income

minus $15,000 expenses (including income taxes)

minus $2500 reserve for emergencies

= $32,500 net income (or 'salary')

Let's say your maximum possible hours of work = 40 hours per week x 52 weeks = 2080 hours

2080 hours

minus 120 hours vacation and training time

minus 80 hours (two weeks) statutory holidays

minus 40 hours (one week) of sick leave

minus 312 hours generating referrals (networking and marketing) (15% of your time)

minus 312 hours administrative office work (15%)

= 1216 hours divided by 52 weeks = 23 hours/week of spiritual direction time on average

(full-time therapists in the United States see 20-30 clients a week on average.)

$50,000 gross expenses (including your salary) divided by 1216 hours = $41/hour fee.

You also need to provide in your fee for the possibility of less clients than 23 hours a week, administrative time and recruitment time being more than 15%, and being sick two weeks not one, so your fee may need to be $45 to $75 per hour or more.

Also, rather than basing your whole income on contact time with clients, you will probably also want to do a fair number of work-shops and retreats which, if set up properly, could bring in a lot of money all at once and thus enable you to lower the fee you charge for individual spiritual counseling sessions.

Another way of calculating hourly fees, based on net income rather than gross income is as follows:

Fee Calculation Based On Net Income

Assuming you want to make what you made in your previous job, here are recommended steps from other professions for coming up with an hourly rate:

1. Calculate your previous weekly take-home pay (your net pay, that is, your pay after deductions). If you know your yearly net pay, divide it by 52.

2. #1 was assuming paid vacation and statutory holidays and sick days, etc. You need to make your calculations based on 47 weeks not 52 weeks. So multiply the amount in # 1 above by 52 and divide by 47.

3. You now also have to cover pension, benefits, and all your overhead (out-of-pocket) expenses that were once covered by your employer. This amounts to 1/3 weekly pay, so add 1/3 of your previous weekly pay to your present weekly pay as calculated in #2 above.

4. You also need to do other things in order to function on your own (e.g., administration, finance, new contacts, new business, logistics, etc.). This will take up at least 15% of your week (and perhaps a lot more at first), so calculate at least 15% of #3 and add to #3.

5. Work out an hourly fee based on the total found in #4. To do this divide #4 by 40 or 35 hours, whatever you worked before.

6. In spiritual direction you may only see two to four clients per day, so you may have to either

   A. adjust your above hourly fee accordingly, that is, charge more per hour than what you calculated above. You may need to gradually raise your present fee to reach this level. It could take several years.

   B. adjust your lifestyle to fit your new income, that is, live more simply

   C. work more hours per week to earn as much as you made before.

7. As suggested previously, you could also set up a number of workshops and retreats which could bring in a lot of money all at once, thus allowing you to supplement your income from doing spiritual direction sessions one-to-one, and possibly allow you to lower the fee you charge for these sessions.

How To Raise Fees

You should consider raising your fees if you don't have enough money coming in to meet your needs (your needs, not your wants), if your expenses have increased, or if your fees are really out-of-line with your level of training and expertise in spiritual counseling. Another possible reason to raise your fees is that, as mentioned before, it might actually be good for your clients.

In raising your fees, mail or email a letter to them beforehand, stating why you have to increase your fee, what the new fee is, and what their options are. Invite them to share their thoughts and feelings on it at the next session. Or, give them a letter at the start of the next session, and then discuss it all with them directly. Do not hand them a letter at the end of a session without any discussion. They may feel disappointed, afraid, or angry, but it is better to calmly deal with this in the session, without getting defensive, than to let them mull over these feelings at home without your input and reassurance.

It is important to be careful about seasonal quitting times. I have found that July and December are typical times when clients quit. Therefore, I will tell them in June that my rates are increasing in October, or tell them in October that my rates are increasing in February, in order to encourage them to keep coming during July and December.

Always remember that you are doing all these things, not just to keep your practice going, but because you care about your clients and believe that spiritual counseling is good for them.

In your letter you could quote what others charge for services that are paid for out-of-pocket by clients, that is, services not covered by Employee Assistance Programs. Only do this if you have actually researched it.

You could also offer to do shorter sessions if they want to continue paying the old rate. Simply pro-rate the hour. As mentioned earlier, you could also just raise fees for new clients, and let the old ones continue at their previous rates. As well, it might be better to raise your fees in small increments. For example, it might be easier for clients to handle it if you raised your fee $2.50 every six months than if you raised it $5.00 once a year.

Before I last raised my fees, I made a pros and cons list as follows:

Pros to Raising Fees:
- My clients are not from the poorer classes. They are middle class and they have the money
- I can offer poorer clients other options so they can pay less and keep coming: shorter sessions, more time between sessions, be in a group
- $50-$90 per month is not too much for most people. Therapists often charge more than this for weekly visits
- If clients quit, then I have more time to look for people who can pay
- I have a doctorate
- I have fifteen years work experience in adult religious education
- If I received $50-$90 per hour I would feel fairly compensated
- Fees are relative and fuzzy: people right out of high school spend two years learning a trade such as massage therapy and then charge $65 per hour
- If I charged more, clients might take it more seriously, put more into it, and get more out of it
- A higher fee would allow me to update my AV resources that clients can borrow for free
- I haven't raised my fees in two years
- I think my clients would understand the fee increase

Cons to Raising Fees:
- A higher fee could cut out poorer people
- A lot of my clients might quit

Based on all this, I decided to raise my fee range. Out of forty clients, two decided to meet with me every second month, one decided to pro-rate the hour to $35 for 50 minutes, and one complained that her hydro bill had just gone up. When I said "so has mine," she got my point that I am not a disembodied spirit, I have bills to pay too, and she agreed to pay within the new range. Everyone else had no problem with the increase. Most of them just said "Oh, okay."

Here is a letter I sent my clients notifying them that I would be raising my fee:

Fee Increase Letter
Dear (Client's Name):
This letter is to let you know that my new fee range for spiritual direction will be $50-$90 starting February 1, 2010. If this causes any financial hardship for you, we can discuss various options at the beginning of our next spiritual direction session.

As you know, I am a married man with children, and have a doctor of ministry degree in spiritual direction. In case any of you wonder what others in similar circumstances to myself charge, I did some research before I set my new fee range. The following are all single or married lay people with Masters degrees or Doctoral degrees doing spiritual direction or Christian counseling or psychological counseling with sensitivity to the spiritual dimension:

Christian Counseling Services of Southwestern Ontario: $69-$99 per hour
Christian Counseling Centre: $80 flat rate per hour
Dr. Ken Wilson: $110 flat rate per hour
Bruce Rutherford, M.S.W.: $80 flat rate per hour
Dr. Rosy Maloche: $90-$120 per hour
Dr. Turner Jorgenson: $95 per hour; $50 per hour for students, seniors, unemployed

Greg Myers, M.A., $70-$100 per hour

(Names have been changed to protect privacy.)

Based on my knowledge of the services provided by some of these people, I believe that the service I provide is of equal or better quality.

If you cannot afford to do spiritual direction within my new fee range and want to keep paying at the same amount as before, we can simply shorten the sessions accordingly:

$35 = 30 minutes

$40 = 40 minutes

$45 = 50 minutes

Thank you very much for your prayers and financial support. I enjoy working with all of you, and will continue to pray for your spiritual growth and offer the best spiritual direction I am capable of.

Sincerely,

Bruce Tallman, Dr. Min.

Member, Spiritual Directors International

Alternatives to Raising Fees

There are many ways to avoid raising your fees. First of all, you could simplify your lifestyle so that you just meet your basic needs. You could scale back your wants and desires.

Secondly, you could earn more by working more hours, or you could cut unnecessary expenses. However, don't consider networking, training, supervision, and professional support through a peer group or business coach, as well as physical and psychological self-care through exercise, meditation, or therapy as "unnecessary."

You could replace costly advertising with low-cost networking. For example, you might want to take a different person to lunch or coffee each week who could refer clients to you.

You could follow the 80/20 rule, that is, that 80% of our results often come from 20% of our effort. Therefore, increase your focus and efforts on the things that currently generate most of your income, and cut down on time-wasters. For example, you could spend less time doing administrative work, and more time generating referrals leading to more meetings with clients.

You could earn more by selling your tapes or books, by running groups where everyone pays less but you receive more than your hourly rate. You could teach classes and facilitate workshops and retreats and do other things to supplement your income so that you can keep going as a full-time spiritual director. These things will also provide much-needed variety and stimulation.

Two final tips about setting your fee. Don't start off too low. It makes it a lot harder to raise your fee to a reasonable rate later. I started too low and it took me about five years to get to a decent rate.

Secondly, someone in a workshop I facilitated said she had heard that some spiritual directors ask their clients to pay them whatever the directee makes per hour in their job. I said I thought that was, frankly, a really dumb idea. Why? Because most people are not self-employed, they receive an hourly rate just for being at the job, whereas as a spiritual director you only get paid when you see clients. So, if your directee was paid $20 per hour and they were the only person you saw that day, at the end of an 8 hour day your directee would have $160 in his or her pocket, and you would have $20 in yours.

How to set and raise fees can be the most delicate and tricky part of your practice, but if you follow the above guidelines, it should take some of the guesswork out of it.

CHAPTER EIGHTEEN

Enjoying Your Practice

Being fulfilled as a full-time spiritual counselor means your work brings you joy. You are doing what your Higher Power has called you to do. Fulfillment does not mean having a lot of clients. On the other hand, having joy but not enough money, so that you don't know if you will be able to continue what you love doing, can interfere with feelings of fulfillment.

True fulfillment means not only doing what you love, but also earning enough, not overworking or underworking, and having clients you are truly helping who genuinely appreciate your efforts for them.

Things To Be Aware Of

The opposite of fulfillment is decline. Here are ten signs your practice is declining:

- constant worry, doubt, and confusion about your practice
- you haven't had any new referrals for months and have no idea how to get things rolling again
- you do know how to get things rolling, but feel no motivation to do them

- your number of clients is steadily going down
- you don't know what your income or expenses have been for the past two months
- you feel constantly bored, exhausted, or burned-out
- you feel isolated
- you are working constantly without any breaks, days off, or holidays
- you do parts of your practice just for the money, even though you hate those parts
- you are jealous of other directors whose work is going well.

The Wrong Way To Work

Fear of not surviving can make a spiritual director work hours they dislike and see clients they don't want to see. This is not good for anyone, as the clients will pick up the director's resentment, uneasiness, and boredom.

Fear that clients won't sign up if you charge as much as you should will prevent you from adequately compensating yourself. Fear that clients will quit prevents you from billing them if they miss sessions without giving you at least twenty-four hours notice.

Fear of not surviving can force you to take on clients when you really don't have enough training to adequately counsel them given their particular needs.

Fear can cause you to resist making helpful changes because you don't want to step out of your comfort zone and call that professional, take that minister or priest to lunch or coffee, or meet with that bishop. Fear can also cause you to accept suffering as part and parcel of running a spiritual direction practice, rather than being proactive and fixing whatever is the cause of the suffering.

All of the above requires you to develop a much deeper trust in God.

Solutions To Overwork

The problem with having totally flexible hours in order to accommodate any client's time schedule is that you can lose control of your own time schedule. You end up working all the time, and if you do have any spare time it becomes filled up with personal tasks: laundry, paying bills, yardwork, etc. There is never any "downtime" and you can become constantly tired.

The solution to this is to set some firm boundaries for you and your clients, that is, schedule in times beforehand when you will not work, for example Friday nights, Saturday nights, all day on Sundays, and Mondays during the day, or whatever is appropriate given your circumstances.

It also helps to take breaks at set times during the day and force yourself to stick to those times. As mentioned earlier, I take four breaks a day: a poetry-reading break in the morning, an astrophysics-reading break at lunch (as well as going for a daily lunch-hour swim or walk), a centering prayer-break (instead of a coffee break) in the afternoon, and a wine-tasting-and-conversation-break when my wife Grace gets home from work. I try to get all personal chores done on one other day each week (usually Mondays) so that Sunday is totally free of work and personal chores.

I believe these breaks improve the quality and effectiveness of my work so that I get more done in less time when I do work.

Trying New Things

Boredom can be a problem in any counseling practice. Listening to people talk about their problems all day can be draining. One solution is to constantly take training in new methods of spiritual counseling and incorporate them into the sessions. Taking risks and trying different approaches that stretch your comfort zone can be exciting. You could try a more contemplative approach and just sit back and wonder at God's strange ways as clients unfold their stories to you. You could try to interject more role-playing and humor into the sessions, and try praying with the client during the sessions if you do not already do that. You could study how to work with a client's dreams, get them to bring their art work or poetry or clay work to sessions, start or end each session with centering prayer or guided imagery, and so on.

One of the greatest solutions to boredom is simply varying what you do. To give you an idea of the creative possibilities and how interesting and fun being a full-time spiritual counselor can be, here is a list of a variety of things I did (by the grace of God) in the first five years of my full-time spiritual direction practice to keep things alive and exciting.

Creative Possibilities

- worked constantly with a case load of forty clients in two cities
- gave a workshop on the impact of Jungian archetypes on spiritual direction in Miami, Florida for Spiritual Directors International
- had an article on this workshop published in *Presence*
- gave a workshop on masculine spirituality for the Men of Today International Men's Conference in Detroit, Michigan
- gave a workshop on archetypes and male spirituality for an ecumenical gathering of church leaders in Gravenhurst, Ontario
- gave a week-long retreat called "An Introduction to Spiritual Direction" at a United Church of Canada retreat center in Naramata, British Columbia. There were forest fires all around us and ashes floating in the air, so that made it really exciting!
- published a book called *Archetypes for Spiritual Direction: Discovering the Heroes Within* (Paulist Press, 2005)
- had an article "Archetypes and Organizational Leadership" published in the *Journal for Organizational Development*
- had numerous articles published in the Spirituality and Ethics section of the *London Free Press*
- did workshops on "Developing a Spiritual Direction Practice" for three different programs that train both Protestant and Catholic spiritual directors
- gave two days of prayer for elementary school staff
- gave talks to women's groups on prayer and spiritual direction
- gave numerous workshops for engaged and married couples
- gave a five day retreat called "Archetypal Christian Living" at Mt. Carmel Spirituality Center in Niagara Falls, Ontario.

• did workshops on "Archetypes and Spiritual Direction" and "Becoming a Full-Time Spiritual Guide: Practical Methods for Making Spiritual Direction or Counseling Your Main Employment" at the Institute of Transpersonal Psychology in Palo Alto, California

Creative Alternatives to Evening Work

Some spiritual counselors need to work evenings, but they don't like how much it takes them away from their families. If one's family life is suffering too much, there are a number of ways to avoid evening work. The first thing is to realize that many people today are free during the day. Not everyone works nine to five: students, housewives, shift workers, retired persons, professionals who set their own hours and work "flex-time," or have flexible lunch hours from as early as 10:30a.m. to as late as 2:30p.m. could all see you during the day.

Many people who work nine to five have one day off during the week. Some people just work part-time mornings or afternoons. You could do half-hour sessions in the morning before people go to work or at lunch if they only get an hour off, or by phone if they have (or can take) thirty minute breaks during the day.

For people who can't come during the day you could see them on Saturdays and take a weekday off yourself to make up for it. For me this is usually Mondays. I used to take Wednesdays off, but found I needed two days off back-to-back. So now I take Sundays and Mondays off, which works well in spiritual direction because these are the same days most clergy take off. If you need to contact them, most of them will not be there on Mondays.

By the way, clergy are more likely than any other group to pursue spiritual direction, for a number of reasons. Their congregation may require it, clergy themselves see the value in it, and they have the continuing education funds to pursue it. My practice has gradually evolved to the point where I now have clergy (and deacons and pastoral ministers) from every major Christian denomination. A warning though: clergy can be very challenging directees as they are usually very theologically well-educated and often very spiritually evolved.

Another option for people who can't come during the day would be to run one or two groups on one weeknight for them. It wouldn't be as ideal as having every evening off, but it would be a good compromise. You could try this experiment—for one month just stop working evening hours completely, force yourself to not give in to people who say they can only come in the evening, and see what happens. If you are disciplined you might find that people *can* come during the day, and you have as much income as before, but now your evenings are free.

Solving Lack And Over-Abundance Problems

Every practice ebbs and flows at different times, causing deflation and inflation in the emotions of the practitioner. There are fallow seasons and growth seasons. My daughter's violin teacher told me that she has boom and bust years. This is common for people in a private practice of any kind. Still, there are several things you can do to survive the down times.

Think of your slow times as gifts; develop several alternate sources of income that you could work on during seasonal slow times for spiritual direction such as December and the summer. You could focus on giving retreats or writing articles or books during these months. Or you might take some new training that you can use to benefit and keep your clients the rest of the year.

A really excellent idea for surviving the down times is to immediately deposit ten percent of whatever you earn into a savings account. You can arrange an automatic deposit through your bank. If times are really tough, you can draw upon this account to tide you over. And if you never have to do that, you can use the money for an extended holiday or maybe even a six month sabbatical. However, you might lose a lot of your clients if you took too much time off.

Running a practice is like running a car—it takes preventive maintenance, attending to things *before* problems develop, cleaning it up so it presents a good image to others, taking out unnecessary baggage (old files, things that aren't working, unnecessary expenses), making seasonal adjustments, putting the right fuel in, tuning it up periodically, and so on.

It's also a good idea to get feedback from others. You could get ideas and support from your supervisor, business coach, mentors, and so on. Even better than a support group composed of other spiritual directors might be a support group composed of non-competing peers such as psychotherapists, reiki masters, massage therapists, and other people who are trying to develop *their* practice, since the same practice-building principles will apply to their situation. Getting together to compare notes will create mutual support and combat isolation. You might even ask them to be on your advisory board, do workshops with them, and refer clients back and forth. As mentioned earlier, you could also form a healing/therapy/spiritual direction center with them.

The opposite extreme from having a problem of lack is having a problem of over-abundance. It may seem unimaginable to most spiritual directors that you could have too many clients, but it does happen. Over-abundance can also be problematic when a non-spiritual direction part of your practice (something you started doing to supplement your income while you built up your spiritual direction practice) becomes a larger and larger part of what you do until it starts to overwhelm your spiritual direction work. For example, since there are so many problematic marriages, the marriage coaching which you started to do as a sideline to support your spiritual direction work, may go from ten percent to fifty percent or more of what you do.

In either case, if you have too many clients, you will need to maintain your boundaries, take breaks and days off, possibly see clients once every six weeks instead of every four weeks, or refer people to others in order to avoid endlessly working.

If you have too many clients you could also encourage group work. Spiritual direction groups could be a solution for poorer people whose workplace does not cover spiritual direction under their Employee Assistance Program or insurance. As you do spiritual direction, consider each client as a possible candidate for a group. Also remember that a "group" can consist of as few as two people other than the spiritual director. *Presence*, the journal of Spiritual Directors International, has numerous articles you could study on how to do group spiritual direction. Check out the back issues.

Keeping Motivated/Saving The Planet

It is always difficult to keep fresh and motivated in any line of work, and spiritual counseling is no different. The main motivator has got to be your ultimate purpose on Earth, whatever that is for you. If it is a desire to heal the planet or spiritually renew the church, that will keep you much more motivated than pursuing the Almighty Dollar. Society puts tremendous pressure on us to reduce everything to dollars and cents, but it is really *not* all about the money. If you know your practice is your means to achieve your calling, then this higher purpose will make the daily tedium manageable, and keep you going.

Secondly, having a positive mental attitude will keep you focused on your goals. Being excited about what you could achieve, and believing you will succeed, will help you overcome any obstacle. Having an expectant attitude helps, because what we focus our thoughts and energy on we tend to draw to us. In this regard, it can help to read inspiring stories about people who have been victorious in spite of great problems. I recently read the story of a man who became a missionary in Africa and led many people to God in spite of having severe cerebral palsy. People like that make you realize that with God all things are indeed possible.

You can also keep yourself motivated by continuing your education. Spending ten percent of your income on new training each year will keep you constantly growing.

Periodically making a list of your past achievements as a spiritual director (workshops, published articles, goals met) can keep your spirits up and make you more aware of your Higher Power's providence in hard times.

You could also reward yourself for completing a tedious task such as keeping your financial records up to date. Each person is motivated by different rewards, so figure out what is rewarding for you: phoning a friend, eating chocolate, playing golf, seeing a movie, etc. You could break your goals down into smaller steps so you could reward yourself more frequently.

Varying your work by writing articles or books or giving talks can also break up the routine. A good mixture of activity will keep things lively.

Basing your practice on love for the people you are serving rather than on fear of not surviving will yield practical results. People will catch your enthusiasm and energy and want to be part of what you are about. On the other hand, fear that you will not survive will paralyze you and result in poor decision-making, and this may eventually do you in.

When you think of your practice or any irritating part of it, try to replace negative thoughts and emotions with positive ones. Give yourself permission to stop judging yourself and your practice for not being perfect, accept what is, try to love all aspects of it, and resolve to make the best of it. The more you love your practice, the more you will work hard at it, and the more profitable it will be, both materially and spiritually.

If you work smarter not harder you can find less stressful ways of reaching your goals, you can discover strategic ways of doing things that require less energy to keep going, and you can eliminate a lot of unnecessary suffering from your work.

You could invite your peers or colleagues to share their success stories over lunch, learn from them and adapt their ideas to your situation. From them you could figure out what resources or training you will need and what action steps will help you to duplicate what they have done.

As many people have said, "luck happens when preparation meets opportunity," and "success equals having a vision, a plan, the courage to carry it out, and lots of sweat."

In the field of psychotherapy it is estimated that twenty percent of therapists leave private practice every year because of a lack of small business skills. This percentage may be even greater in the field of spiritual counseling.

As a spiritual counselor it is indispensable to remember that prosperity and service to the world are intertwined—as your practice succeeds you help the spiritual health of individuals and this affects the whole spiritual counseling field which in turn affects the whole spiritual health of our society and our world.

The key things to remember are that your Higher Power is the ground of your practice, prayer fertilizes it, and you water it and tend it with your actions. Ethics and spiritual values (love, trust, service, putting people first) will cause your practice to grow and blossom like a precious flower.

So your Higher Power, prayer, and you are all essential in building your ministry. You have to do what is humanly possible and live in trust that God will do what is humanly impossible, keeping ever in mind that what the world needs now is love, sweet love, and so spiritual directors and counselors have a key role to play in transforming not only the lives of individuals, but our whole planet.

Summary of Some Key Ideas & Helpful Tips

To make your spiritual direction practice soar, take the following action steps:

- pray every day that your Higher Power will send you clients
- thank your Higher Power every day for the clients you already have been given
- pray every day for the spiritual growth of your clients
- trust that referrals follow service/love
- have a written mission statement for your practice that is meaningful to you and energizes you
- have a plan for fulfilling your mission
- pray your mission statement and plan every day
- tell others about your mission
- read the two books on how to build a therapy practice recommended in "Practice Building Resources." I have summarized most of the key points here, but there are details I didn't include
- make your mission statement into positive, personal affirmations you say to yourself often

- eliminate aggressive marketing and rely on attraction marketing
- eliminate any negative ideas about being an entrepreneur or running a small business
- know your strong points as a spiritual counselor
- know what makes you unique as a spiritual counselor (your niche)
- be able to give examples of how people have benefitted from your work
- put together spiritual options/packages people can choose from
- know what your fee needs to be to survive
- know how to raise your fee without losing clients
- be able to give clients affordable other options if they can't afford your regular fee
- keep track of all expenses and income
- know what expenses you can write off
- have written office policies that you and your clients follow closely
- get back to people who leave a voicemail or email as soon as possible—within twenty-four hours
- if someone wants to try spiritual direction, try to meet with them the same day or as soon as possible (people can change their minds quickly)
- the first two visits are the most crucial
- hospitality is key. People are often nervous about going to spiritual counseling for the first time
- always thank people who refer clients to you, and keep track of where referrals come from
- call clients the night before to remind them of appointments, especially for Mondays
- try to set up tentative appointments with people who say "I'll get back to you." It is easier for them to not get back to you than to call you and cancel a tentative appointment you have set up.

- dress casually but professionally (particularly at home—no slippers or jeans)
- be flexible with your appointments. Be prepared to work evenings and Saturdays
- become a full-time spiritual counselor slowly. Keep building a part-time practice until you are ready to go full-time
- have several sources of income besides spiritual counseling: writing, workshops, retreats, etc.
- get some training in supervision, so spiritual counseling interns can pay you for supervision
- do a two hour weekly review and planning session: review possible contacts and presentations, brainstorm plans for upcoming weeks and months
- ask clients to pay as they go. Don't let debt accumulate
- keep your skills up with workshops, books, journals. For example, subscribe to *Presence*, the journal of Spiritual Directors International, and read a page or two a day
- set up a spiritual counselors support group in your area. Pray together, do peer supervision, swap ideas on how to do spiritual counseling and how to run a spiritual counseling practice
- surround yourself with people who want you to succeed
- if clients are coming from a distance, remind them that the time in the car can help them prepare for spiritual counseling. It's a good time to pray, do a spiritual inventory, think of what they want to work on in the session. They can also go over the session on their way back
- if you are doing a workshop, have participants do a written evaluation at the end which includes their name, position, and whether or not you can quote them as you line up future workshops
- constantly let others know you have openings you are looking to fill. Otherwise people will think you are full and won't refer people

- identify the type of ideal client you want to work with. This focuses your search.
- develop an email list of potential clients and email them spiritually helpful ideas regularly
- invite people to free previews of your work, that is, group meetings at your office where you have people sample different ways of praying, or discuss different themes of spirituality
- give clients what they want, not what you think they need. For example, they may want to have more self-esteem, but you want to teach them the Enneagram
- remember, clients are primarily interested in benefits they will get, therefore design all your brochures and advertising around the benefits of spiritual counseling
- get sponsored by organizations if possible
- make sure you can clearly and concisely explain your basic message of what you do and the main benefits of your services in 30 seconds or less
- constantly educate people about spiritual direction
- seminaries and theological schools often require their students to have a spiritual director and make lists of spiritual directors available to their students. See if you can get on the list
- work ecumenically. Many clergy and others within a tradition see it as an advantage to do spiritual direction with someone outside their tradition. Clergy and clergy spouses in particular may want the privacy and anonymity that someone outside their tradition provides
- ponder ways of connecting with the 80% of the population that attends no religious services
- get a web site. There are people who can design an inexpensive web site for you and give you software so you can make changes yourself
- regularly update your web site with new workshops you are offering—let clients know this

- get a business coach, reread this book several times, or peruse the business section of your local bookstore for adaptable ideas
- at the first session discuss with the client how they can benefit the most from spiritual counseling
- get a supervisor or at least a peer supervision group
- have your own spiritual director and note how it feels to be a client when you meet with him/her
- have an advisory board to support and encourage you and keep you honest ethically
- cultivate relationships with professionals (doctors, lawyers, massage therapists, etc) who interact with a lot of other people and could refer some of them to you
- publish or self-publish a book and include a copy in the price of workshops you do
- know when the slow times of the year are for you, and use this time to do things that will bring future referrals or income from other sources: writing, workshops, etc.
- get a full listing in Spiritual Directors International "Seek and Find" Guide
- fix anything you don't like about your practice
- be aware of future trends that will affect your practice
- balance work, play, and relationships
- remember: your practice starts at home. Put your loved ones first. Otherwise you will have a busy practice and strife at home
- if a client doesn't show up, see it as an opportunity to do things that will generate even more clients in the future. Ask "How can I best use this free time?"
- offer free sessions if people can't pay
- donate ten percent of your work for free ("pro bono") and trust that God will provide for you
- operate out of an abundance mentality not a scarcity mentality

- run your practice based on love for your clients not on the fear of not having enough money
- figure out which of the ideas in this book will work for you and apply them
- be selective and prioritize the things in this book. Don't try to do everything in this book at once or you will drive yourself crazy
- remember: it may take three to five years to build a thriving full-time practice
- use your blog, Twitter, Facebook, and YouTube to attract seekers. Enter posts on your blog and tweets on Twitter daily or as often as possible
- study the book on social media networking recommended in "Practice Building Resources"
- always remember as you build your practice that you are doing this not to get rich, but because you love others, and you really believe in the power of spiritual direction to help people. You are doing all this to serve God and others.
- always remember: it is God, prayer, ethics, your efforts, and living spiritual values that build your practice.

Practice Building Resources

Note: Grodzki and Browning's books are about how to build a psychotherapy private practice. Grodzki gives you the grand overview and the Brownings give you the minutest details. Both are highly recommended as follow-up reading to this book. I have summarized many of their key points in this book but still, both these books would be a valuable supplemental read. You should be able to order all four books recommended below through the Internet at reduced prices.

Browning, Charles and Beverley. *Private Practice Handbook.* Duncliff's International: Los Alamitos, California. (2000). ISBN: 0-911663-77-0.

Grodzki, Lynn. *Building Your Ideal Private Practice: How to Love What You Do and Be Highly Profitable Too!* W.W. Norton & Company: New York (2000). ISBN: 0-393-70331-2.

Lakein, Alan. *How to Get Control of Your Time and Life.* New American Library: New York (1996)

Zarella, Dan. *The Social Media Marketing Book.* O'Reilly Media Inc: Sebastopol, California (2010) ISBN: 978-0-596-80660-6

Spiritual Directors International. *Guidelines For Ethical Conduct.* Email: office@sdiworld.org.

About the Author

Bruce Tallman completed a Doctor of Ministry degree in Spiritual Direction from the Graduate Theological Foundation in 2003. Paulist Press published his first book *Archetypes for Spiritual Direction: Discovering the Heroes Within* in 2005. He has been in full-time spiritual direction since 2002. For fourteen years before that he was the director of two adult religious education centers for the Roman Catholic Diocese of London, Ontario. Besides his spiritual direction work, Bruce gives workshops and retreats across North America. Grace and Bruce live in London and have three amazing children: Hailey, Brandon, and Alana. To bring his workshops "Archetypes for Spiritual Direction," "Empowered Spirituality," or "Finding Seekers" to your group, contact:

btallman@rogers.com
519-433-0981
www.brucetallman.com

" Discernment of Spirits
   Interior movements
            - thoughts
            - Imaginings
            - emotions
            - inclinations
            - desires
            - Feelings
            - repulsions
            - attractions
   Becoming sensitive to these
movements, reflecting on them
   + understanding where
they come from + where they
lead us.

CPSIA information can be obtained
at www.ICGtesting.com
Printed in the USA
LVHW040123231218
601183LV00001B/240

9 781937 002084